HEALING: QUESTIONS AND ANSWERS FOR THOSE WHO MOURN

Visit our web site at
WWW.ALBAHOUSE.ORG

or call 1-800-343-2522 (ALBA)
and request current catalog

HEALING:
Questions and Answers for Those Who Mourn

Rev. Terence P. Curley, D.Min.

ALBA·HOUSE   NEW·YORK

SOCIETY OF ST. PAUL, 2187 VICTORY BLVD., STATEN ISLAND, NEW YORK 10314

ST PAULS

Library of Congress Cataloging-in-Publication Data

Curley, Terence P., 1944-
  Healing: questions and answers for those who mourn / Terence P. Curley.
    p. cm.
  Includes bibliographical references.
  ISBN 0-8189-0905-6 (alk. paper)
    1. Church work with the bereaved—Catholic Church. 2. Bereavement—
Religious aspects—Catholic Church. 3. Grief—Religious aspects—Catholic
Church. I. Title.

  BX2347.8.B47 C86 2001
  248.8'6—dc21
                                                          2001041388

Nihil Obstat:
Rev. Alfred E. McBride O.Praem, PhD

Imprimatur:
✠ Bernard Cardinal Law
July 23, 2001

The Nihil Obstat and Imprimatur are official declarations
that a book or pamphlet is free of doctrinal or moral
error. No implication is contained therein that those
who have granted the Nihil Obstat and Imprimatur agree
with the contents, opinions or statements expressed.

Produced and designed in the United States of America by the
Fathers and Brothers of the Society of St. Paul,
2187 Victory Boulevard, Staten Island, New York 10314-6603,
as part of their communications apostolate.

ISBN: 0-8189-0905-6

Printing Information:

Current Printing - first digit   1   2   3   4   5   6   7   8   9   10

Year of Current Printing - first year shown

2002   2003   2004   2005   2006   2007   2008   2009   2010

Dedication

To Bernard Francis Cardinal Law

*With deep gratitude for your compassion
and Pastoral Leadership for the
Ministry of Consolation*

Table of Contents

Section Four: Afterword

Section Five: Appendices

Preface

Healing: Questions and Answers for Those Who Mourn was written specifically for those who are experiencing the suffering which stems from life's separations and losses. It is the product of two decades of working with the bereaved. During that span of time I have often noted that those who are suffering losses need some basic information to assist them while they grieve.

It is unfortunate that most of the literature surrounding grief is too academic. There are just too many terms and theories to really help people who need to know in readable terms what is happening in their lives. Using a question-answer technique, I felt, would provide a brief explanation for the chaos, spiritual upheaval, and emotional concerns they are experiencing in their grief. The explanations are provided in this format so that the reader can more easily understand how his/her Christian faith speaks to them in their loss. The ultimate goal of this formation is to bring them closer to Jesus as their Lord.

The plan of this little work is threefold. It will look at the initial phase of loss—the time of the death, funeral, and period immediately following the loss—and the early emotional reactions and responses during this critical period. The second phase to be looked at is the transition between the past and the present. This phase usually takes place approximately two to three months after the loss. The emptiness has to be filled with ways to spiritually "sort out" what is happening in our lives. The final phase to be considered is the period of re-adjustment. Now after six months of grieving how ready are we to continue life without our loved one? How do we remember them and find meaning in life? These all-important questions along with many others will be explored in these pages.

My hope is that this little work will assist you with a spirituality for your experience of loss. If ever we need to be comforted by the Lord's presence it is when we suffer the loss of a loved one.

Terence P. Curley

Introduction

Our society is not structured for those who grieve. Separation and loss are avoided and denied at all costs. This is especially true when we suffer the loss of a loved one in death. People may be concerned and offer condolences without the ability to appreciate the long-term effects loss has on the grief-stricken.

It is not uncommon for co-workers, friends, and even parishioners to shy away from the reality of loss. This makes good grief work all the more difficult for the bereaved. It also does not allow those who mourn to find peace from their relationships which could be invaluable resources for healing.

Bereavement is a time of chaos and upheaval. It can lead us into darkness or bring us into a new and enlightened faith.

This little work is a miniature catechesis for those who mourn. Our immediate concern is to assist you in your journey through grief and to help you to move from darkness to light. At the same time we are also helping ourselves to prepare for losses in our own lives. It is inevitable that all of us will be among those who grieve as we live out our lives.

Catechesis

Catechesis is an elementary instruction in the Christian faith that touches virtually every aspect of our life. It provides us with that formation in Christ necessary for those who desire to follow the Lord more closely. There are specific moments in our lives when catechesis is especially needed. All of the rites of passage necessitate formation in Christ in order for us to find meaning as our lives change.

When we mourn we need to appreciate what is really happening to us physically, emotionally, and especially spiritually. We need to understand ways we can grow spiritually as we hunger and thirst for meaning in what we are experiencing.

In Matthew's Gospel we hear in the words of one of the Beatitudes from Jesus' Sermon on the Mount our earliest catechesis or teaching regarding grief: "Blessed are those who mourn for they shall be comforted."

Rebuilding Trust

In many ways our worlds are shattered when we lose a loved one. Life can lose its meaning for us. In order to heal we need to trust and believe again in life. We need to establish a new spiritual relationship with our loved one who has died. In realizing that life is not ended, merely changed, we have to begin the work of re-establishing our relationships with our loved one on a new spiritual level.

Our Lord's teaching reminds all who grieve that we live with the bright promise of immortality. Our society treats life as if it has ended. Our trust in God assures us that "life is changed, not ended. When the body of our earthly dwelling lies in death we gain an everlasting dwelling place in heaven."

Turning Points

A crisis is a turning point in our lives. How well we do in going through a crisis has far reaching effects on our spiritual well-being. We need to be prepared to handle life's crises, especially those associated with loss, with some kind of plan. Not to prepare ourselves only makes our grieving all the more difficult.

When a major loss such as death occurs we need a context in which to express our grief. Our faith is the resource which brings expression and meaning to our lives at such a critical time. Trust in a loving God who promises to be with us always is a healthy response to loss.

Parish Communities and Catechesis

The Apostle St. Paul constantly catechized in his ministry and letters to the early communities of faith. Through him they were made aware of how their Christian faith applies to everything in life. Among other things, Paul taught that the members of the community are responsible for consoling and ministering to one another at all times: "Let the word of Christ dwell in you richly; teach and admonish each other with all wisdom; sing psalms and hymns and spiritual songs to God with thankfulness in your hearts" (Col 3:16).

Our parish bulletins like Paul's apostolic letters are ways of teaching the members of our faith community about events such as death which need to be placed into the context or perspective of faith.

Call to Teach the Good News

The Christian community is invited to catechize, that is, to teach the Good News to others by word and example. In so doing it strengthens its own faith response and is able to witness in concrete ways to those in need of God's love and concern. Those who are grieving need to have members of the community willing to be present with them during their time of loss.

Pastoral visitation programs for the bereaved are a form of catechetical ministry. The pastoral visitor represents the concern and love of the greater parish community. In many instances these visitors are "ambassadors for Christ." There may also be other members of the believing community who would be willing to be spiritual guides or loving listeners for those who mourn.

Serving One Another

While we minister we are also preparing ourselves for crises we may have to face in our own lives. Our ministry gives us a perspective for a more effective spiritual way of coping with our losses. Having helped others to experience the broader faith perspective we are able to see beyond our own personal situation. We give our sorrows to the Lord, and in doing so we realize that death has no power over us.

St. Augustine once remarked that faith is powerfully expressed when tears are shed in front of a crucifix. Christians need to join their sufferings and sorrows to those of the Lord. We too must take the road to Calvary. Our Lord's words and example inspire us to walk that lonely road with him, especially while we grieve.

Reassurances

As mourners, we need to be reassured while we grieve that we are not alone. We need to know that there is a meaning and a purpose behind what we are suffering. The parish is that sacred place that provides the necessary spiritual support.

Caring in the Community

A pastoral visitor recently left with a bereaved person a little holy card with the following message written by St. Francis de Sales.

Do not look forward in fear
To the changes of life;
Rather look to them with full
Hope that as they arise,
God, whose very own you are,
Will lead you safely through
All things; and when you cannot
Stand it, will carry you
In His arms.

Do not fear what may
Happen tomorrow; the same
Everlasting Father who cared
For you today will take care
Of you then and every day.
He will either shield you
From suffering, or will give you
Unfailing strength to bear it.
Be at peace and put aside
All anxious thoughts and
Imaginations.

Healing Images

There are many healing images we can turn to while we grieve. Scripture and Tradition teach us that we are God's children. He will never leave us. When we feel lost or abandoned, he is our Good Shepherd who goes out of his way to seek us out and bring us back home again. He weeps with us when we are sad as he wept with Martha and Mary on the loss of their brother Lazarus. He felt the pain of the widow of Nain and came to her aid. He will help us cope in what may well be the most difficult time of our life.

Biblical Abbreviations

OLD TESTAMENT

Genesis	Gn	Nehemiah	Ne	Baruch	Ba
Exodus	Ex	Tobit	Tb	Ezekiel	Ezk
Leviticus	Lv	Judith	Jdt	Daniel	Dn
Numbers	Nb	Esther	Est	Hosea	Ho
Deuteronomy	Dt	1 Maccabees	1 M	Joel	Jl
Joshua	Jos	2 Maccabees	2 M	Amos	Am
Judges	Jg	Job	Jb	Obadiah	Ob
Ruth	Rt	Psalms	Ps	Jonah	Jon
1 Samuel	1 S	Proverbs	Pr	Micah	Mi
2 Samuel	2 S	Ecclesiastes	Ec	Nahum	Na
1 Kings	1 K	Song of Songs	Sg	Habakkuk	Hab
2 Kings	2 K	Wisdom	Ws	Zephaniah	Zp
1 Chronicles	1 Ch	Sirach	Si	Haggai	Hg
2 Chronicles	2 Ch	Isaiah	Is	Malachi	Ml
Ezra	Ezr	Jeremiah	Jr	Zechariah	Zc
		Lamentations	Lm		

NEW TESTAMENT

Matthew	Mt	Ephesians	Eph	Hebrews	Heb
Mark	Mk	Philippians	Ph	James	Jm
Luke	Lk	Colossians	Col	1 Peter	1 P
John	Jn	1 Thessalonians	1 Th	2 Peter	2 P
Acts	Ac	2 Thessalonians	2 Th	1 John	1 Jn
Romans	Rm	1 Timothy	1 Tm	2 John	2 Jn
1 Corinthians	1 Cor	2 Timothy	2 Tm	3 John	3 Jn
2 Corinthians	2 Cor	Titus	Tt	Jude	Jude
Galatians	Gal	Philemon	Phm	Revelation	Rv

When We First Face Loss

Spiritual Help for Those Who Grieve

Does the Church have a special concern for those who are mourning?

Since the earliest days of the Church there has been concern for those who are grief-stricken. Widows and orphans are always to be taken care of in the community. In our day this ministry to the bereaved is called the Ministry of Consolation.

To what does the Ministry of Consolation refer?

The Ministry of Consolation is an expression of care on the part of the parish community. It includes liturgical and pastoral assistance at the time of the loss, help in planning the funeral, and so forth. Following the funeral this ministry provides support groups, retreats, special liturgies and pastoral visits to the bereaved.

Is there a need for guidance when loss occurs?

There is need for considerable support and occasional guidance while we grieve. Religious faith is always necessary if we are to find hope and consolation in the midst of the chaos we are experiencing.

Can mistakes be made while grieving?

Denial of our loss, avoidance or refusal to face life without our loved one can lead to more serious physical, emotional and even spiritual difficulties.

What is necessary for good grief?

We need to experience and express our loss realistically. We then need to let go of our attachments to the past and finally we need to recover and reinvest in our lives once again as we continue on our journey to the Kingdom.

How can I express my grief in a society that says I should get over it?

Unfortunately our society shows no sensitivity to those who are grieving. The parish community often provides the only safe place for the bereaved to tell and retell their story of loss.

How necessary is it to tell our story of loss?

Everyone's sense of loss is unique. We do, however, share some common characteristics with others. All of us need to tell the story of our lives in order to accept the fact that the loss is real. We need to find a place where we feel free to tell our story to those who are willing to listen in a compassionate way.

What influences the Christian in the way he or she tells the story?

The Christian is able to relate their suffering to the way Jesus suffered. In our grief we walk with the Lord in his way of the cross and, in so doing, we join our grief with his.

Where do we turn for guidance while we grieve?

Support groups, special seminars for the bereaved and your local parish are all very helpful.

Are there spiritual books available to help one to better understand the experience of loss?

Many publications about grief exist, many of which are

listed in the Bibliography of this book. Most of these are available at your local Catholic bookstore or directly from the publisher.

Are there spiritual figures in the Church on whom I can rely for help with my grief?

Mary as the Mother of Consolation, or Mother of Sorrows, is an excellent model for us to rely on in our grief. Devotion to her has brought peace and consolation to millions down through the ages.

Are there special devotions for those who are suffering a loss?

The Church always remembers those who have died in every celebration of the Mass. Other devotions include the Way of the Cross in which we join our sufferings to those of our Lord as we walk with him. The Rosary is a very suitable prayer for those who are grieving. We find especially helpful the sorrowful mysteries which are expressions of the depth of Christ's love for us as demonstrated by the way he suffered and died for us.

Do the Scriptures help those who are suffering a loss?

"The Lord is close to the broken-hearted" is a theme we find in many of the Psalms. The Psalms were the prayers Jesus prayed. He found them helpful. We will too.

What Psalms are the most helpful?

The Psalms of Lamentation are cries from the heart which give voice to our feelings in an especially effective way. But there are many others that express hope and confidence in God which are equally helpful. The 23rd Psalm has always been a favorite of many.

Understanding Grief

*What initial reactions can we expect to have when we hear
about the loss of a loved one?*

When we first hear about such a loss, especially if it is sudden, we may cry out, "Oh, no!" We are shocked. Such a reaction may be addressed to those around us and to God. We may want to avoid or deny what has happened.

*How can we describe a person's emotional state when the
news of a loved one's death is reported?*

Very often depending upon the degree of bonding or love there is shock and numbness at the news. This is often accompanied by denial when the initial news takes hold.

*Does our relationship with the deceased make a difference
with the way we respond?*

It certainly does. There is what is known as high grief and low grief. High grief is when we have an intense bond with the loved one such as a mother, father, wife, or husband. A bond that is not so intense would be one with a co-worker or acquaintance. This bond could generate a low grief reaction.

*How does the Church view grief when it happens to the
community?*

St. Paul tells us that when "one member suffers in the community we all suffer." There must be a prayerful response for the deceased and the family. As Christians we are called to minister to one another in our community. We share in a communal faith. As a community we build the new Jerusalem.

What is a good definition for grief?

Grief is the deep mental anguish or sorrow we feel over the loss of a loved one. How we view our losses very much colors our way of grieving. Grieving is the process whereby we undergo a change in our relationship with a loved one—from one based on physical presence to that of remembering a loved one and reestablishing a spiritual relationship with them.

Is grief an illness?

Grief is a natural occurrence in our lives. It is not an illness. Grief only becomes an illness if we are unable to cope with it. This could lead to depression. Grief unchecked and unaddressed can manifest itself through various physical, mental and emotional ailments.

What are some of the symptoms associated with grief?

There are a variety of symptoms associated with loss. Everyone grieves in a personal way. What one person may experience another may not. There may be feelings of emptiness, searching and yearning to be with the loved one. Anger, guilt, feelings of abandonment and other emotional symptoms are often noted in varying degrees.

Does crying indicate a lack of faith?

Crying does not indicate a lack of faith. Rather it is an expression of a bond of love. Jesus wept at the death of his friend Lazarus. Crying provides a catharsis or cleansing of our emotions. When we express ourselves in tears we are adjusting to our loss in a very appropriate way. It is not healthy to suppress our feelings. As we grieve we should allow and encourage the expression of feelings. Often those who are grieving wait for permission from those around them to truly express how they feel.

Is there a time limit for grief?

There really is no time limit for grief. There are general ways to describe how we adjust and go through the various phases of grief.

What are the phases of grief?

Initially we have an *intense experience of separation.* This begins when we hear the news of the death and it lasts approximately six to eight weeks. The next phase is a *period of transition* during which the initial symptoms of shock or numbness wear off. This phase usually lasts about three months in which the bereaved have to continue doing "grief work." The third phase takes another three months and is the *time of readjustment.* This is the time when the bereaved begin to adjust to the loss and initiate new outlooks and frameworks in their lives.

What does "grief work" mean?

Grief work is the process of performing certain tasks which help us to express and accept our loss. The tasks of grief work are spiritual and emotional. Spiritually, we need to express through prayer and rituals our innermost feelings associated with loss. Emotionally, we need to accept that our lives are different due to the loss. We need to learn to cope with this major change.

What are some of the "tasks" of grief work?

Some of the tasks associated with grief are:
1. Accepting that the loss has really happened.
2. Expressing our emotions. This means being able to recognize and give voice to our innermost thoughts and feelings.
3. Adjusting to a new way of life without the loved one.
4. Developing a new spiritual relationship with the loved

one. Re-investing energy in new ways of remembering.

Do those who are grieving need reassurances?

It is not uncommon for those who are grieving to have certain misgivings about themselves. They need to be reassured that they are going through a normal experience in life. They are not going insane. The disorientation they experience does not necessarily indicate illness.

Is it necessary to become familiar with symptoms while we grieve?

The more familiar we are with the usual course of grief the better we are able to cope with our losses. Becoming familiar with the symptoms often brings the peace of mind sought after by those who are grieving. Fear of being psychologically or spiritually ill may be dispelled.

Symptoms of Grief

What are some of the normal emotional responses associated with grief?

Some of the initial normal responses associated with grief may include: feelings of anger, sadness, loneliness, shock, tiredness, numbness, abandonment, anxiety, yearning to see the lost loved one, emancipation, relief, irritability, guilt, and emptiness. This is not an exhaustive list. These and other symptoms correctly tell us about the overall disorientation and disruption in our lives.

What are some of the normal physical reactions with grief?

During the initial phase of grief certain bodily symptoms may manifest themselves. Some of the most noticeable include: an emptiness in the stomach, tightness or constricted feelings in the chest and throat, a sensitivity to noise, shortness of breath, muscular weakness, a lack of energy, and dry mouth.

What are some of the ways of thinking affected by grief?

The way we think may be affected by our grief. Among the most apparent are denial, confusion, a preoccupation with the loss, a sense of experiencing the presence of the deceased through auditory and/or visual hallucinations. Most commonly we suffer from "distractibility." We are distracted in the way we perceive what is happening. We cannot seem to focus our attention. Intense grief has shocked the conscious mind. These initial defenses are normal. They give us time to come to grips with the shock and loss. Only when they linger for a good length of time is there an indication of difficulty.

What are some of the behavior changes affected by grief?

When we grieve we know that we are not acting in our usual manner. We are not really ourselves. We need to reflect and talk about what is happening to us. Some of the things we may notice include:

> trouble sleeping,
> changes in appetite,
> withdrawal from others,
> denial of memories about the loved one,
> restlessness,
> over activity,
> crying,
> searching for or yearning to be with the deceased loved one,
> visiting places frequented in the past with the deceased,

idealizing the memory of the deceased,
inability to let go of the deceased's possessions,
calling out to the deceased. These and other symptoms indicate just how much life has changed.

What are some of the spiritual changes affected by grief?

Grief is a chaotic time and occasionally our religious life is even affected. Anger and hurt may become misdirected toward God. It may also be directed toward the deceased. "Why did you leave me?" "How could you let this happen?"

Are there positive spiritual changes occurring while we grieve?

As we begin to accept our loss we see life differently. Our sense of the eternal may become much more real. Our hope of seeing our loved one again fits into our belief in a heavenly reunion. Our commitment to our own life's journey culminating in the Kingdom inspires us to change the way we are living. We may find ourselves more detached from material things in order to become more attached to God. We begin to see, though still dimly, that there is more to our existence than just the here and now.

We often hear the phrase "the grieving process." What is this process?

The grieving process involves putting our lives back together by dealing with painful memories, expressing our emotions and admitting that we are struggling as we are trying to sort things out in our lives. Our struggle may be with anger, emptiness, and guilt among other things. This process is a necessary part of working through our bereavement.

What is involved in determining the outcome of our grieving process?

Everyone's grief is unique. This is because so much depends on our earliest childhood experiences, significant losses later in our lives, crises before the loss, any emotional illness we may have, and our relationship with the deceased. The person's entire spiritual and emotional life will determine the outcome.

What other factors affect the grief outcome?

Some time to prepare ourselves before the loss can make it easier for us to cope at the time of separation. How we view life and its meaning is very important to our acceptance of the loss. Our spiritual ways of hoping and trusting in the eternal love of God are very significant for the way we process our grief. If there is a faith foundation in place then we already have a pathway through grief before us.

Spiritual Needs

What are some of the needs facing those who grieve?

The grief-stricken need to go through a process whereby they learn to let go of the loved one's physical presence and move toward relating to them in a different way.

Does remembering a loved one mean that they are only a memory?

Remembrance, in the religious understanding of the word, means "to make present." Jesus, in instituting the Eucharist tells us to "Do this in remembrance of me." In other words, "In doing this, realize that I am present with you." A remembrance or memorial is more than a memory; it involves being in touch and present in a new spiritual way. While we may not see our loved ones physically, they are near. Just as we do not see those in another room yet know they are there, so we know that our loved ones are with us, though in a different way.

How do we go about remembering our loved ones?

We remember our loved ones in faith when we develop a spiritual relationship with them. This relationship is fostered by prayer. Our dialogue with God assures us of the hope for eternal life. Our belief is in the communion of saints.

What do we believe about life and death?

One of the prayers in the Funeral Mass states: "Lord, for your faithful people life is changed, not ended. When the body of our earthly dwelling lies in death we gain an everlasting dwelling place in heaven." Death is our entrance into eternal life. We believe that life is eternal. In believing life is eternal we know that death is only a doorway we all pass through.

How important is prayer while I grieve?

Prayer is essential for good grief. It is the way we are able to accept and continue our life as persons who have hope. Our hope is in eternal life and a heavenly reunion with our loved ones. This is the comforting image which brings healing for us while we grieve. Prayer raises our consciousness so we can see more clearly that while there is change there is no end.

Is it important to pray for those who have died?

God's love is mediated through his justice. When we die

we see ourselves as we really are. We need forgiveness for our sins. During our time of purgation, as we wait for the fullness of the Kingdom to be revealed, the faithful on earth pray for the faithful departed. As we pray for our loved ones we not only help ourselves see more clearly but we help our deceased loved ones who share our communion with God.

What do I hope will happen while I pray during this time of loss?

A primary concern is that I will be able to know my true feelings and express them toward my deceased loved one and even to God. In this way I am placing my emotions in the context of faith, hope, and love as I struggle to learn how to love and trust again.

I find it difficult to go to church since the funeral.

This is a remark we often hear in pastoral counseling. Sometimes it is difficult to go to places where our most loving and intimate memories were formed. Yet to go through grief it is necessary that we do so. When the bereaved finally confront their feelings, they often remark on how special and close they feel in that sacred setting. While church was the place where we may have said our last "good-bye," it was and also is the place where we are born in the spirit. The atmosphere of the church reaffirms our faith and reminds us of our goal, which is eternal life.

Is it a lack of faith not to be able to pray?

Not being able to pray stems from our sense of loss. The fatigue, shock, numbness, anger, and guilt we may feel are all obstacles to our relationship with God and everyone else. We must first look at what is happening to us before we jump to conclusions about our faith. Prayer takes many forms. We may *feel* confused and distracted in our prayer life, yet our crying out and pain can also be a very pure form of prayer when we open ourselves to God's love in our mourning.

What do I do when I find myself unable to pray?

We may need to look to our style of prayer. Our concentration is affected by our grief. We need to calm down. Perhaps we need to be less formal in our prayer. We may need to search for more peaceful settings to help us pray. If prayer is an offering then we offer what we have—our grief, confusion, and anger. In offering these raw emotions we ask to be cleansed and strengthened to change them.

What about our overall feeling of powerlessness?

It is necessary to face our very real powerlessness in this circumstance. Our acceptance of this feeling and our surrendering to God will bring inner peace. In acknowledging our powerlessness we gain power because we know that we cannot go it alone but need God's help to transform us.

How can I begin to accept God's will?

It is not easy to immediately accept our losses. Accepting what has happened and trusting in God is the process we have to go through. We may at first cry out in anger and sorrow. Eventually we will come to realize that God has not set out to harm or punish us. We know that life is not confined to this existence. We are merely in the anteroom of eternity. Just as we would not live our lives in hallways we need to move on to fulfill God's will.

What images of Jesus can help me with my spiritual needs?

Jesus took on all human suffering. This includes the grief you now feel. When Lazarus died, Jesus wept. He also must have wept at the death of his foster father, St. Joseph. To this day the Church honors St. Joseph as the patron of a happy death because of the presence of Jesus and Mary at his side when he died. Jesus, the foster son of Joseph and the friend of Lazarus, shared our emotions and losses. He knows how we feel and doesn't condemn our feelings. Rather, he shares them with us and transforms them.

Faith Resources

Can you name some of the best resources in religious faith for grief?

We are blessed as a Church with a rich history of spiritual writings that speak to every aspect of life. Our best living resource remains the Scriptures when our feelings are in need of direction and transformation. They speak to our times of sadness as well as joy. In the lives of the saints we find that the same struggles we are going through often defined their sanctity as they trusted in the Lord. Spiritual practices abound for us as ways to express and accept our losses: the Mass, prayer, spiritual reading and devotions such as the Way of the Cross and the Rosary.

Name some of the spiritual practices which help us while we grieve.

If we look first to the Liturgy we find that, in every celebration of the Mass, there is always a remembrance of the dead. We sincerely believe in the communion of saints and are constantly reminded of those who have gone before us marked with the sign of faith. In Holy Communion we are brought into intimate union with Christ the head of his Church both on earth and in heaven, where our loved ones await us.

Is the practice of a "month's mind Mass" helpful for the bereaved?

The practice of celebrating a Mass for the deceased one month after their death is very beneficial for the family. At this time the initial phase of numbness and shock is beginning to wear off and the family is coming to grips with their loss. When all that they have endured is placed into the context of faith, the members of the family derive great consolation and peace.

Can retreats or days of recollection assist the bereaved?

Retreats and days of recollection when they are geared to the bereaved are very helpful. Certain themes such as loneliness, longing, anger, guilt and others may be explored in a setting that is both confidential and prayerful. Others who are grieving also participate. This often creates a community focus for the losses each one is experiencing at the time. Such practices can help individuals re-integrate their lives into the life of the Church while coming to a better acceptance and understanding of what they are going through.

Do parishes have special days for the bereaved?

Many parishes designate the month of November for prayer not only for all the departed, but also for the bereaved. On the feast of All Souls parishes invite families to a special liturgy of remembrance for those who have died during that year. Candles and flowers are often important items used in the liturgy to help the bereaved express their loss. A parish book of remembrances lists the names of all who have died. Such special liturgies set aside time to be especially mindful of our new relationship with the deceased.

Is there any value to having a parish support group?

Very often more is accomplished in joining a group than seeing someone individually. A parish based support group explores both spiritual and secular themes important for bereavement. These groups can be a great catalyst for healing.

Is a support group therapy?

A grief support group is helpful in the healing process. It is not meant to provide psychological therapy. Rather it is a gathering of persons who come together not only to share their pain but to gain strength for getting on with their lives in spite of their loss. Therapy groups are for those who are in need of more in-depth treatment. Such groups are led by counselors, psychologists, and social workers.

If I decide to join a group what should I look for?

It is always important to ask the right questions. Some of these might be: What are the credentials of the facilitators of the group? Is there confidentiality? Will I feel as though I am on the spot? What type of a commitment do I have to make? Are there themes relating to spiritual growth being explored by the group? What is the comfort level of the group?

Will I be judged by the feelings I express when I go to the group?

The group should always be non-judgmental. Feelings of emptiness, helplessness and even rage towards God for what has happened may be expressed. No one is there to tell you what to feel. How you feel as you try to work through this loss is confidential and everyone is encouraged to express their emotions freely.

How do Church groups vary from secular groups?

The parish group employs many of the same procedures as a secular group. Information about the grieving process and all of the difficulties you may expect to encounter may be very similar. The parish group helps the bereaved to tap into the rich resources of faith and assists the participants in placing the loss into a faith perspective. The Church group draws on the rich traditions and writings of the Church to help members realize where grief fits into their lives as Christians.

What about social groups for the bereaved?

Social groups are very different from support groups. They are valuable if all someone is looking for is companionship or friendship. In the social group themes and insights about grief are rarely offered. Joining a social group may be the natural next step after participating in a support group.

How are both social and support groups valuable for the bereaved?

Both are very helpful as they give the bereaved "permission" to work through their grief. We need others to help us as grief work is very strenuous. It is not easy to face our losses. Others provide the support which is so necessary.

What are some of the themes provided by parish-based groups?

Some of the themes may include: (1) The symptoms of grief; (2) How the tasks of grief work; (3) Ways of coping utilizing our faith; (4) Utilizing faith resources found in Church spirituality and writings and especially the Scriptures on an ongoing basis.

What other factors are important to keep in mind for support groups?

The timing of a group is very important. Many groups set their calendars to include sessions before and around the holidays. This is very helpful with coping during those seasons which bring back so many memories of loved ones.

What else is very important to know about parish-based groups?

Parish-based groups relate to areas of faith and belief. Very often such groups have prayer services which help the bereaved to rebuild trust. Loving and trusting again takes time and support. Committing our emotions to God's care is a significant step in letting go and reconnecting with God in new ways. In our death-denying culture where people are expected to "move on" with their lives very quickly parish support groups acknowledge that healing takes time and they offer a place not tied to any artificial time frame imposed by society. Parish support groups are a safe place to share and gain support during and after our losses.

Healing Rituals

Do rituals have a significant role for the bereaved?
Rituals, whether they are personal or communal, are very important for those who are grieving.

How do we express rituals?
We express our rituals by word and action. Religious rituals are a body of ceremonies or actions which help us express our connectedness with God and one another. Through these rituals we communicate our beliefs, our hopes and our concerns in a formal way.

How are rituals vehicles for healing?
Rituals are actions which bring our feelings to our conscious awareness. They help us concretize our ambiguous feelings. Rituals help us let go of the past and welcome the future. They also signify what is beyond our worldly comprehension and make our loved ones present in unique ways for us.

Do rituals help with the grieving process?
Rituals provide guidance and show people how to grieve. Through gestures, words, signs and symbols the reality of loss is given necessary expression. In so doing our perceptions are changed and placed into a faith perspective.

How do rituals and rites help my faith?
Ritual actions connect our human love with the power of God's love. They enable us to participate and minister to one another in a ceremonial fashion. Liturgical rituals make present God's love in unique and meaningful ways.

How do rituals assist us in expressing our feelings?

They do so in a variety of ways. For example, the ritual of jotting down our thoughts about a loved one, keeping a journal, writing poetry, creating a piece of art, and composing a song are all ways of directing our innermost intimate feelings in ways that heal and transform our emotions.

Do rituals provide structure for our grief?

Rituals help us to find meaning in what we are experiencing. We need to sort out our feelings. Rituals provide a way of doing this. Family gatherings and conversations which help us reminisce all bring healing. Families need to perform these rituals. Special family based rituals such as gatherings on anniversaries, birthdays and other events assist us in redefining our relationships following a loss.

Funerals

What do funerals accomplish for those who are mourning?

Meaningful funeral rites provide many benefits. Through them mourners receive spiritual and psychological assistance. Funerals provide us with a fitting way to express our faith and our love for the deceased. They not only assist our deceased on their journey but also assist those left behind.

Is it possible to have burial without Christian funeral rituals?

Unfortunately, in a secular society it is possible to omit religious funerals. This can happen at times when a Christians outlives his/her generation. If remaining relatives are not religious they often give in to our death-denying culture and choose to not have a religious funeral for the deceased. People of faith should make arrangements ahead of time to ensure that there will be a Christian funeral for them if it appears that religion is not a value to those who may be left to bury them.

How can the omission of a religious funeral be avoided?

It is necessary for us as Christians in our day not to take anything for granted. Provisions may be made in a person's will for Christian burial. The executor/executrix of the will ought to be aware of our wishes.

What is the name of the way funerals are celebrated in the Catholic Church?

In the Catholic Church the name of the ritual used for the burial of a Christian is the *Order of Christian Funerals*. This rite has been in effect since 1989. It beautifully reflects our faith while being focused on healing and hope.

What are some of the ways in which funerals help mourners?

Funerals are the introduction to the public expression of grief. We call this mourning. They provide a focus for the bereaved in their grief. The ritual calls for participation by both the bereaved and the minister. Prayers are offered for the deceased Christian as well as for those who mourn their passing.

How does the Order of Christian Funerals act as a healing vehicle?

When Christians gather together they are called to use signs and symbols in ways which bring consolation. The participation and ministry offered by the ritual demonstrate love, provide us with an opportunity to say good-bye in a loving way, and strengthen our hope for our eventual heavenly reunion.

What is the best way to understand the funeral journey?

The funeral rites reflect the idea of a journey: from death to life, from earth to heaven. In this procession or journey we begin immediately following the death of a loved one right up until his or her burial with various prayers and rites. At the end of their earthly journey, we accompany our deceased loved ones with prayers that express our faith, our hope and our love.

What are the ritual moments for a Catholic funeral?

The moments may be listed as:
1. Prayers After Death (OCF, ##101-108),
2. Gathering Together in the Presence of the Body (OCF, ##101-111),
3. The Vigil (OCF, ##51-97, 243-263),
4. The Funeral Liturgy (OCF, ##128-203, 264-315), and
5. The Rite of Committal (OCF, ##204-233, 316-341, 405-408).

How are the "Prayers After Death" conducted?

The prayers at the time of the death bring peace and consolation to those who are grieving. Family and friends may gather at the health-care facility or the home. According to the ritual, special prayers are offered at this most intense time of loss. These prayers assist those who are mourning to place the immediate loss into the context of prayer.

How does the "Gathering Together in the Presence of the Body" assist the mourners?

These prayers are a very healing experience as the family and friends view the body of the deceased for the first time since it has been prepared for burial. These prayers may be offered at the parish church or in the funeral home depending upon the decision for the place for the wake or Vigil.

Why do we use the term "Vigil"?

"Vigil" is a term used in the revised funeral rites. It replaces the term "wake." From the earliest days Christians have watched and waited for the return of the Lord. Christians express this vigilance in special prayers offered in this the first formal liturgical moment in the funeral journey. It is highly recommended that the parish church replace the funeral parlor or chapel for prayers for the deceased Christian. Many parishes are accommodating this request from parishioners.

What is the focus of the "Funeral Liturgy"?

The funeral liturgy is best celebrated within the Mass. This is the heart of all of the funeral rites. The Funeral Mass places the Christian's life into the context of the paschal mystery of the death and resurrection of Christ.

How can we appreciate "The Rite of Committal"?

This is the ritual moment when we say our last good-byes before the body of the deceased is committed to the grave. This is a very difficult time for family and friends to let go. Our presence at the grave brings solace when we rely on God's love to bring us through the dark night of our grief.

How do we say farewell during the ritual moments according to the Order of Christian Funerals?

Our prayerful participation in the ritual is the way we say

farewell. There is a practice of reading a farewell during the final commendation. This is done at the end of the Mass before the final recessional. There are opinions surfacing that a more suitable place for this farewell would be at the vigil or wake service.

What does the funeral farewell consist of in the Catholic Church?

The farewell is the time when we take leave of the deceased's body. It is a time when we say good-bye in the context of faith. It is not meant to be a eulogy. A eulogy is an extolling of human accomplishments. A farewell is an extolling of what God has given the person the ability to accomplish in this world, how they used their gifts and talents in serving God and his creation. The focus here is on how the deceased lived the Christian life, how they embodied the Word of God in their life.

Is there value to the farewell which is given at funerals?

The funeral farewell is a vehicle which stimulates our recollections about the deceased loved one. It expresses feelings and acts as a catalyst for the expressing of emotions. This, as with the entire funeral, promotes a realization that the loved one while separate from us is not gone. It also is a prayerful way of fostering the development of a new relationship in faith. The farewell is a reminder to all present that life is changed in the Spirit.

How can we appreciate the signs and symbols used in funerals?

The signs and symbols used in funerals illustrate our faith journey beginning in Baptism. The self-same symbols are used at the end of our earthly life. The signs and symbols are integral parts of the tapestry which is our lives as

Christians. They are sign posts of what is significant in life.

What are the symbols we should note at the funeral?

Symbols which recall the Christian's baptism such as the white garment (now the funeral pall), the lighted candle (now the Paschal Candle), the water (now the holy water sprinkling the casket), and the prayers by name for the deceased Christian all signify that they have been signed with the seal of salvation. The prayers of petition according to the ritual recall the sacramental life of the Christian.

What does the pall signify at the funeral?

The pall reflects the clothing of the person at Baptism when a white garment was used to designate the new life of the Christian. We remember in this ritual action the words of Baptism: "See in this white garment the outward sign of your Christian dignity. Bring that dignity unstained into the everlasting life of heaven."

How important is the white garment?

We are told in the Rite of Baptism to bring our garment "unstained into the everlasting life of heaven." It is both a symbol of our innocence and a charge for our parents/ Godparents to live lives of faith to be imitated by the baptized as they journey through life.

Who places the pall over the casket in the gathering area of the church?

The ritual allows for family and friends to place the pall over the casket. Just as family members clothed us as an infant so too does the family and Christian community clothe us on our journey to eternity.

How does the Order of Christian Funerals describe the meaning of the funeral pall?

The ritual tells us that according to custom in the local community the pall may be placed over the coffin when it is received into the church. It further tells us that this is a sign of Christian dignity. When we use the pall it also signifies that all are equal in the eyes of God (*Order of Christian Funerals*, #38). Each of us in receiving the baptismal garment were charged with a mission. That mission is now ended. We will be judged on how well we did.

What other symbols are placed on the casket?

A family Bible may be placed over the casket draped with the white pall. This highlights the importance of the Word of God for the Christian as well as family memories attached to the Bible. When we are faithful to the Word and its message we are led to eternal life.

Are there other symbols which may be placed on the pall?

The family may decide to place a crucifix or rosary beads. Both of these sacred objects may have been an intrinsic part of the deceased Christian's life. The symbol shall hold some special Christian meaning for the deceased.

Is there a lack of faith when tears are shed at the funeral?

The liturgy is meant to help those who are mourning to release emotions. A rigid approach only stultifies emotions. It is appropriate and human to express ourselves while we mourn.

Do secular symbols have a place in a religious funeral?

These symbols do contribute to the funeral. We remember that a loved one was a member of certain associations, national organizations, a veteran, etc. This is all part of the personal journey. While recognizing the merit of these symbols the Church makes some important distinctions about their use.

Does the Church exclude these symbols?

By treating the funeral as a process or procession, the Church is not excluding them, rather it designates times when certain other symbols should be paramount.

What does the ritual tell us about the symbols?

The *Order of Christian Funerals* tells us that only Christian symbols may rest or be placed near the casket during the funeral liturgy. At that time any other symbols, for example national flags, or the flags or insignia of associations are not to be part of the funeral liturgy (see #38). The Church is here acknowledging that the true Christian life transcends all secular symbols and focuses on the eternal.

When are the secular symbols used?

The secular symbols may be used before the casket enters the church. The importance of the pall and other sacred symbols has to be respected. The secular symbols may be replaced after the coffin has been taken from the church (*Order of Christian Funerals*, #132).

What is the central theme of the funeral liturgy?

The Funeral Mass has the sacred theme of uniting our lives with the paschal mystery. We celebrate life in relation to Jesus' life, death and resurrection.

How can we become more familiar with how to celebrate a Catholic funeral?

There are many ways parishes can prepare us for funerals. This preparation is known as a catechesis or instruction. At the same time along with information we are given better ways to form our faith and trust in God. A good place to start this instruction is to go to the *Order of Christian Funerals.* There are also publications available which help us to understand the new ritual and its moments.

Where in the ritual is a good place to further my understanding about the funeral?

In the *Order of Christian Funerals* there is the General Introduction. This Introduction highlights many important aspects for ministry and participation.

Does the introduction mention specific roles in celebrating the funeral?

The Introduction gives excellent insights into the role of (a) the Community and Ministry of Consolation, (b) the Liturgical Ministries, and (c) the Mourners and Friends and their spiritual/psychological needs.

Does the Introduction mention symbols?

It mentions other symbols such as (a) the Easter Candle and other candles, (b) Holy Water, (c) Incense, and (d) Liturgical Colors.

Why is there an Easter or Paschal Candle present at a Funeral Mass?

The Easter Candle reminds us that we live in Christ's presence who is the Light of the World, our Resurrection and our Life. Again the Baptismal ritual is recalled by the lighted candle. Parents and Godparents at the beginning of the Christian's journey are handed the candle lighted from the Paschal Candle. They are told "keep this light burning brightly" (OCF, #35).

How do we understand the use of Holy Water?

Holy Water also recalls our Baptism. The saving waters of Baptism are recalled by the Holy Water sprinkled on the casket at the funeral. Using the same symbol at the end of the journey also serves as a reminder of the cleansing waters of faith and now bids the deceased farewell as he or she continues on their journey (OCF, #36).

What is the meaning of incense?

Incense is a sign of the community's prayers for the deceased Christian. Our prayers are being raised up to the presence of God. Again at the funeral the incense is a sign of farewell as our prayers join the deceased in hope of their being raised up (OCF, #37).

What colors of vestments are permitted at the Funeral Mass?

The liturgical colors are again signs of the hope we have in eternal life. In the United States, white, violet, or black vestments may be worn during the funeral rites (OCF, #39). These colors reflect the consciousness of the communities where the funeral takes place. For the most part violet and black vestments that symbolized suffering and loss have given way to white vestments symbolizing resurrection and new life.

Have there been any major changes in the Catholic Funeral ritual?

In 1997 there was an appendix to the *Order of Christian Funerals* permitting cremation. The appendix outlines how the Church prefers this to be done. Cremation is allowed when there is a firm belief that this choice was made for those reasons that did not involve a denial of our belief that there will be a resurrection of the body in the end times.

Why was cremation not accepted by the Church in the past?

There are two major reasons why the Church did not accept cremation in the past. The first was that for a very long time the Church was a very small minority within a large pagan culture. That culture for the most part did not hold to belief in the afterlife. For them, cremation was an appropriate burial method. By contrast Christians saw their identity intimately connected to the afterlife and the resurrection of the body. Respect for the body for them seemed to require a proper burial.

What bears evidence to the early Christians' reverence for the body?

The catacombs, as a sacred place for burial, bears witness to the reverence the early Christians had for the body when most in their society were cremated.

When did the practice of cremation cease in the Roman Empire?

Around the fourth century with the conversion of Constantine. In 789, Charlemagne made it a capital offense to follow the pagan ritual for cremating the body. For the next thousand years cremation was abandoned as a practice in Europe.

When was the prohibition for cremation changed?

The prohibition for cremation was changed during the Second Vatican Council. The choice to cremate must not be based on beliefs contrary to the Christian conviction of the sanctity of the body and its eventual resurrection at the last judgment.

When did major changes begin to take place with this option?

In 1969, changes in prayers at the time of burial were

made, but it was not until the appendix to the *Order of Christian Funerals* in 1997 that we note some important guidelines for the funeral and burial of the cremains.

How does this change in the appendix to the funeral rite emphasize respect for the cremated remains of the body?

The ritual instructs us that the remains of the cremated body should be treated with the same respect we would show the human body from which they originate. It further states that a worthy vessel containing the remains ought to be used for transport and final disposition (OCF, #417).

How should the cremains (ashes) be disposed of?

The ritual states that the cremains are to be buried in a grave or entombed in a mausoleum or columbarium. The practice of scattering the remains on the sea, from the air, or on the ground, or keeping the remains in the home of relatives or friends is not what the Church considers a reverent disposition. The ritual further states that whenever possible a plaque or stone with the deceased's Christian name should be adopted (OCF, #417).

When should the cremation take place?

It is recommended that the cremation take place after the funeral liturgy (OCF, #418).

May a funeral liturgy be celebrated in the presence of cremated remains?

The Congregation for Divine Worship issued a special indult permitting the celebration of the funeral liturgy including the Mass in the presence of cremated remains. There are special provisions allowing this practice according to the *Code of Canon Law* and the guidelines of the local bishop. Appendix 2 of the *Order of Christian Funerals* explains other liturgical procedures for the celebration (OCF, #426).

Does the ritual mention the need for catechesis about the presence of the body for the funeral rites?

Pastors are encouraged to make particular efforts to preserve the teaching that the Church prefers and urges that the body of the deceased be present at the funeral rites as the human body better expresses the values which the Church affirms (OCF, ##413-414).

Do some people wonder about the resurrection of the body in light of this change?

Resurrection must be placed in its proper context. St. Paul's words on this matter give us an insight into the manner of our future resurrection: "Perhaps someone will say, 'How can the dead be raised? What kind of bodies will they have?' You fool! What you sow doesn't come to life unless it dies! What you sow isn't your body as it will be—it's a bare kernel, like wheat or something of that sort. God gives it the body He's chosen for it.... This is the way it is with the resurrection of the dead. What is perishable when it is sown is imperishable when it is raised. What is sown in dishonor is raised in glory. What is sown in weakness is raised in power. A physical body is sown, a spiritual body is raised.... Just as we've borne the image of the man of dust, so too we'll bear the image of the man from Heaven" (1 Cor 15:35-49).

Why is it so difficult for us to conceptualize the resurrection?

Pope Paul VI had this to say, reminding us that our hope is to share one day in a resurrection similar to that of our Lord: "Jesus rose again in the same body He has from the Blessed Virgin, but in a new condition, vivified by a new and immortal animation, which imposes on Christ's flesh the laws and energies of the Spirit.... this new reality... is so far above our capacities of knowledge and even imagination that it is necessary to make room for it in our minds through faith."

How did Jesus' body change in the resurrection?

First of all, it was glorified, transfigured. It could no longer suffer. It was able to pass through doors and walls undeterred. It could appear and disappear instantly. In his risen body, Jesus was able to be seen and touched. He could talk and walk and eat.

In the Apostle's Creed we profess our belief in the resurrection of the body. Does the manner of burial influence this belief?

Resurrection never presumes an intact or non-cremated body. Resurrection is the glorification of our earthly body. God's power to bring this about is absolute.

SECTION TWO

Changes and Passages While We Mourn

Building Spiritual Structures to Aid Us in Our Bereavement

In this section we will explore questions often raised after the initial phase of loss. Approximately three months after the loss new concerns surface. There is a hunger and thirst for meaning as the grieving process continues. This search is for spiritual meaning about the deceased's life and our own as well. We need ways which bring hope and consolation. A spiritual framework for loss is necessary for a healthy and holy way of going through bereavement.

Describe the necessity for a spiritual structure for grief.

> Grief is oftentimes chaotic. We need to find purposeful ways to navigate our journey through grief. Having a spiritual framework allows us to move forward toward the goal of eternal life and communion with the whole Church.

What role does prayer play in our time of bereavement?

> Prayer is our way of relating with God. We express our innermost self when we communicate with God. There are many ways to pray which run the gamut from crying out to sublime contemplation.

How can prayer assist us while we mourn?

> We receive the strength of God's love whenever we pray.

It also orients us in our outlook toward life eternal. We become more aware that we are on a journey to God's heavenly Kingdom.

Are there insights from Scripture which strengthen our convictions about eternal life?

If we listen to St. Paul's powerful words, we realize that he had no doubt about the matter: "If Christ wasn't raised from the dead then everything we proclaimed is in vain, and so is your faith. Moreover we will have been found to be false witnesses against God, for we have testified that God raised Christ, whom He couldn't have raised if the dead in fact are not raised. For if the dead are not raised, then Christ wasn't raised either; and if Christ wasn't raised your faith is worthless and you are still in your sins. If our hope in Christ is for this life only, we are the most pitiable of men. As it is, Christ *was* raised from the dead, the first fruits of those who have died" (1 Cor 15:14-20).

How can prayer assist us while we mourn?

Through prayer we more easily see our life in terms of eternity and are often moved to alter our priorities. We become aware of our journey toward the Kingdom of God, and in this awareness our life is changed.

What framework does St. Paul give us for our grieving?

St. Paul continually reminds us of the consequences of our membership in the Body of Christ, the Church. He writes: "If one member suffers, all the members suffer" (1 Cor 12:26, OCF, #8).

Who are called to participate and minister in the Body of Christ?

Everyone is called to the Ministry of Consolation. Priests, deacons, religious, lay persons are all called to comfort those who are mourning. Even while we mourn we must be ready to console others who are likewise grieving.

Why do we need the Church to work through our losses?

At the center of the Church's life is the proclamation that Jesus is the one "who was handed over to death for our sins and raised to life to restore us to fellowship with God" (Rm 4:25). This fellowship that we have with God in the Church gives power to all the Church's actions which are performed in Jesus' name. The Church is the spiritual structure through which Christ heals and restores our broken spirits.

Does the experience of loss deepen our need for the Church?

Going through grief creates many changes and transformations. Our grief can be converted into grace. An entirely new outlook may occur. This conversion brings with it the need to worship and find peace in the sacramental life of the Church.

How does the Eucharistic sacrifice strengthen our bond or ties with one another and God?

We are renewed and nourished by the celebration of Christ's Passover from death to life. Our union is strengthened. "Because there is one bread, we who are many, are one body, for we all partake of the one bread" (1 Cor 10:17, OCF, #3). The Eucharist sets us apart while bonding us together with both the Church triumphant in heaven and the Church struggling in the world.

How does St. Paul place our grief into a context of faith?

St. Paul's theology of grief gives us the spiritual structure we need to be clear in our minds about death. His letter to the Thessalonians brings healing to us in our communities of faith. "We would have you be clear about those who sleep in death, brothers; otherwise you might yield to grief, like those who have no hope. For if we believe that Jesus died and rose again, then through Jesus God will also bring with him those who have fallen asleep in death" (1 Th 4:13-14).

What does St. Paul mean when he writes about being clear about those who sleep in death?

St. Paul is reminding us that we cannot be like the pagans whose grief is motivated by despair. When we grieve we always keep in mind our hope in the resurrection. We grieve the immediate separation from our loved ones, not an irreversible loss. While our loved ones are not present to us physically, they are still with us. Just as one rises from sleep at the dawn of a new day, so we will rise from the dead at the dawn of our resurrection to life in eternity.

How do Christians find consolation?

Our consolation is found in the promise of eternal life. As we await the return of the Lord there is comfort in our grief. We await our reunion with those who have died and gone on before us. St. Paul tells us how the Lord himself "will come down from heaven at the word of command, at the sound of the trumpet; and those who have died in Christ will rise first" (1 Th 4:16).

As we await the heavenly reunion on the last day what must we do?

We need to be present to one another. We look forward to that time when we will be reunited with those whom we love. As St. Paul writes: "Then we, the living, the survivors, will be caught up with them (those who have died in Christ) in the clouds to meet the Lord in the air. Thenceforth we shall be with the Lord unceasingly. Console one another with this message" (1 Th 4:17).

How did early Christians remember those who died?

There are many references to gathering together for the Eucharist and the singing of psalms. In the community there was the strong belief that caring for the dead was best accomplished through prayer. Prayers are offered for those who have gone to the Paradise of the Shepherd. In the Acts of the Apostles we are given glimpses of a caring, supporting community that is very present to one another in their sufferings.

How did the early Christians express their mourning?

Early Christians did not cry out in despair. Rather they sang psalms and hymns expressing their innermost feelings of thanks and confidence in God.

What does St. Augustine tell us is the way to express our love for our deceased loved ones?

St. Augustine emphasized that prayer is what is really best for those who have died. He even wrote a treatise entitled: *The Care to be Taken for the Dead.* None of the faithful departed are to be excluded from our prayers.

How do the Scriptures help us sort out our emotions?

The Scriptures were written from a faith perspective and

must be read with the eyes of faith in the Resurrection. Then we will see that all of the Scriptures point to hope and salvation. The most emotional of the direct responses to grief are found in the Psalms. Most often the approach of the psalmist is to lament or cry out to God in his suffering and to beg for a sign that he could hold onto. That sign was clearly given for all time in the Resurrection. Cries of lament during times of grief and anxiety are common in the Old Testament. When a person suffered the emotional turmoil of grief a prayer or psalm of lament came spontaneously to their lips.

Can we benefit while we mourn from the way these psalms of lamentation are structured?

We most definitely can, especially when we make these psalms our own. They help us sort through our emotions and to imitate Jesus who also prayed these psalms.

Prayer Models

How are these psalms structured?

These psalms, written as an ongoing dialogue with God in which the psalmist's frequently repressed emotions are identified and laid bare, are composed in the following way (this outline may help you to compose your own psalm as a prayer):

1. *The psalmist calls upon God*: This may be a short cry. While we grieve we often cry out in anguish and deep sorrow. This cry expresses our human hurt and releases our innermost emotions.

2. *The psalmist gives voice to his complaint*: We may

lament about something that has occurred in the community. It could be any loss, the loss of a loved one, a disaster or disease. The lament brings all this to the fore. It may describe many aspects of the chaos in one's life due to a loss.

3. *The psalmist turns in trust to God*: In the psalms of lamentation we notice that there is an actual turning to God and a change from the initial outpouring of grief. This illustrates the beginning of a resolution or an acceptance of the loss. This rebuilding of trust is accomplished when we recall how much God has always loved us in the past.

4. *The psalmist asks or petitions for deliverance*: In Psalm 6:3-5 we visualize and can identify how desperate life can be and how much we need assistance. "Have pity on me, O Lord, for I am languishing; heal me, O Lord, for my body is in terror.... Return, O Lord, save my life; in your mercy rescue me."

Are the laments dirges?

Certainly not. They help us to realize that there is a framework or structure for our prayer. They are a cry from the heart for things to improve. They are a pure form of prayer.

What is the distinction between a lamentation and a lament?

A lamentation is an expression of grief over a loss which cannot be reversed. That accounts for the dirge. On the other hand, a lament includes an appeal to God to change what has occurred. When we grieve we pray for both acceptance and change. We lament and seek God's healing presence and assistance.

How do these psalms turn our grief into prayer?

In Psalm 6:2-6 we pray with the psalmist sharing his faith that things will change, answers will be given, and spirits will be healed:

> I am wearied with sighing;
>> every night I flood my bed with tears;
> I drench my couch with my weeping....
>> My eyes are dimmed with sorrow;
> The Lord has heard my supplication;
>> The Lord has accepted my prayer.

What other psalms are especially helpful for grief?

There are many psalms that deal with grief. Probably the most popular is Psalm 23. This Psalm guides us as we journey "through the dark valley." It encourages us to trust as we address the Lord as our Shepherd. The reason for its popularity is immediately apparent when we read it. Here we walk with the psalmist through the dark valley of loss and grief. Yet we know, even in the suffocating darkness, we are not alone. Our Lord walks with us.

Do the psalms help us deal with our anger during times of grief?

The following excerpt from Psalm 22 is very helpful for this important task of grief work.

> My God, my God, why have you forsaken me,
>> far from my prayer, from the words of my cry?
> O my God, I cry out by day, and you answer not;
>> by night, and there is no relief for me
>> (vv. 2-3).

These words identify the initial pain and anger before deciding to turn to God for strength. There is an actual crying or yelling out to God.

> "Be not far from me, for I am in distress;
>   be near, for I have no one to help me."

How does identifying with the psalmist's anger help?

Our anger and feelings of loss are given voice by the psalmist who obviously felt at one time as we do now. He gives expression to the religious reality of our situation and enables us to voice our own true feelings. We can own them as normal and not irreverent to God. We acknowledge the pain of our human condition while acknowledging our need for God. We can move on in grief after this.

How do psalms speak to the very intense feeling of longing?

Longing is one of the most prevalent emotions associated with grief. There is a searching and yearning for our departed loved one. The psalms place longing into a religious context. Psalms 42, 63, 84 and 143 all share this theme of longing/yearning.

Psalm 42

> As the deer longs for the running waters,
>   so my soul longs for you, O God.
> Athirst is my soul for God, the Living God.
>   When shall I go and behold the face of God?
> My tears are food day and night,
>   As they say to me day after day,
>   "Where is your God?"

The final part of the Psalm renews trust in God.

> Why are you so downcast, O my soul?
> Why do you sigh within me?
> Hope in God! For I shall again be thanking you,
> in the presence of my Savior and my God.

As we long for God we long to be at home with God and our loved ones who have moved on.

New Testament

What prayer from the New Testament brings healing and strength for the bereaved?

The Our Father (Mt 6:9-13) is the prayer for Christians journeying toward the Kingdom. It is addressed to God the Father whose providential care we especially need while we grieve.

How is the Our Father meaningful for the grief-stricken?

There are a series of petitions in this prayer. Becoming aware of what these petitions mean as they are applied to grief is very healing. In acknowledging God and praying for the Kingdom we put our lives and losses into the perspective of the heavenly Kingdom that will come. We ask God to be with us every day and to feed us with his bread of steadfast love.

What does the word "petition" mean?

"Petition" is from the Latin verb meaning "to seek." When we petition God, we are seeking or asking, desiring, acknowledging and even expecting God's intervention.

Prayers

The Our Father (Mt 6:9-13)

There are seven petitions in this prayer to God the Father that can apply to those who are mourning. The following are the seven petitions with a brief grief commentary for offering the prayer.

"Our Father who art in heaven..."

Petition 1. "Hallowed be thy name": *God alone is the Holy One. We are created in his image and want to be holy. Holiness brings healing and wholeness. We seek this wholeness amidst our brokenness and grief.*

Petition 2. "Thy Kingdom come": *Even while grieving we must seek first the Kingdom of God. If we seek first the Kingdom then all else follows. We ask that the Kingdom's peace, light, and joy be upon us.*

Petition 3. "Thy will be done on earth as it is in heaven": *We seek, not our will, but the will of God. We ask for the grace to accept. Acceptance brings healing and hope. There is so much more to learn about God's will. This petition helps us to seek the eternal, the infinite as the measure of our earthly existence.*

Petition 4. "Give us this day our daily bread": *Hunger and thirst is very evident when we experience loss. We need to be strengthened every day and fed spiritual food to be able to continue on our journey to the Kingdom.*

Petition 5. "And forgive us our trespasses as we forgive those who trespass against us": *We ask for openness to the healing love of God. In my irritability and even anger help me to love and forgive those who hurt me by their indifference to my loss. Help me to be aware of the many relationships around me.*

Petition 6. "And lead us not into temptation": *Help me to not avoid and deny my loss. Rather deliver me from the chaos. Convert my grief into a grace which will change me while I mourn.*

Petition 7. "But deliver us from evil": *This last petition is a prayer for deliverance for the whole human family. We pray that we will be delivered from all those structures of evil which are not life giving. In our grief we ask to always be steadfast in our faith as members of the Body of Christ and in the communion of saints.*

How does the prayer of deliverance offered at Mass bring healing?

The prayer at the end of the Our Father seeks from God a peace which the world cannot give. We pray for a peace which consoles and comforts our souls. *"Deliver us, Lord, from every evil and grant us peace in our day. In your mercy keep us free from sin and protect us from all anxiety, as we wait in joyful hope for the coming of our Savior, Jesus Christ."*

The Threshold of Hope

What do the Beatitudes remind us about concerning our life's journey?

The Beatitudes are a constant reminder that we live on the threshold of hope. We are children of the Kingdom. Our real home is in the Kingdom of Heaven. As the Word of God the Beatitudes bring us a peace which the world cannot give.

Do the Beatitudes in the New Testament speak to our grief?

The Beatitudes are found within Jesus' Sermon on the

Mount. These sayings of Jesus are an example of our earliest catechesis about how to live our lives and hope for the Kingdom. They are very important for developing a spirituality especially while we grieve. They provide a healing structure for our meditation and prayer.

What is the best way to think about the Beatitudes?

The Beatitudes are a gateway to the Kingdom. They are eight virtues which are necessary for us if we are to live our lives as God wishes us to live them. They bring hope to the poor and broken-hearted and remind us of the bright promise of immortality awaiting us in the Kingdom of Heaven.

What did Jesus do for us when he gave us the Beatitudes?

When Jesus preached his Sermon on the Mount he summarized for us the essence of his teaching. As the core of the spiritual formation of his disciples, the Beatitudes are clear indications of how Jesus expects us to live our lives. They bring us a hope and joy that no one can take from us (Jn 16:22).

What do the Beatitudes accomplish for us?

The Beatitudes guide us in ways which help us to act in accordance with God's will and under his special care. They link us with a spirituality which gives purpose to our lives. They draw us out of ourselves and call us into the service of others.

How do the images of hope in the Beatitudes speak to our grief?

How well we connect with the Kingdom will measure our spiritual growth. The images of hope given in the Beatitudes bring healing especially for those suffering loss.

They provide us with the realization that life is eternal. It is our own humanness which limits our view of life. These eternal words break through our physical limitations.

How can the Beatitudes affect our outlook toward life while we mourn?

The Beatitudes show us how the Kingdom of God is operative in our lives. They are a kind of frame around the picture of our lives. They show us how close we are to God and he to us. Cultivating this spiritual sense of the presence of God and his blessing is essential for managing our losses.

How can we experience the healing power of the Beatitudes?

When we meditate on the Beatitudes especially during critical moments something happens to our spirit. We find ourselves on the mountainside listening to words full of hope. Each Beatitude has a message for us which relates to our story of loss.

Do the Beatitudes give us direction?

Yes, indeed. Even though we do not always want to admit it, we need guidance. Keeping ourselves focused on the eternal Kingdom helps us to live more fully in the present moment. The Beatitudes set up a structure we need to truly develop the necessary spiritual instruments to find meaning and place our loss into the context of hope. When we explore each Beatitude we will find a message for us how to steer our emotions in ways that really matter.

What version of the Beatitudes is helpful for us while we mourn?

The version of the Beatitudes found in Matthew's Gospel (Mt 5:3-12) is very suitable as a way of prayerfully reflecting on our journey through grief.

Beatitudes for Those Who Mourn

How blessed are the poor in spirit. The reign of God is theirs.

Blessed are we when we empty ourselves. Happy are we when we surrender to God. Our turning toward the Lord brings us beyond ourselves. We admit our own powerlessness, depending on God to lift us up.

Blessed are those who mourn. They shall be consoled.

We are not alone when we grieve. Amidst our feelings of abandonment we realize that we can go through the dark valley safely. It is the Lord who gives us direction and peace.

Blessed are the meek. They shall inherit the land.

We are given a sense of self-worth while our self-esteem is low. The Lord will validate us as we cry out for meaning. Being meek while we mourn means accepting our dependence upon God and his plan for our life.

Blessed are they who hunger and thirst for holiness. They shall have their fill.

We hunger and yearn to be with those whom we love. We feel so incomplete. Holiness is the wholeness we yearn for and need. In this Beatitude we are blessed with the promise of fulfillment even amidst our dryness. The living waters are available for us.

Blessed are they who show mercy. Mercy shall be theirs.

The compassion we give will be given to us. Our good works in being kind and consoling towards others bring us peace. We show the living presence of God in our lives in our mercy-filled encounters with others.

Blessed are the single-hearted. They shall see God.

It is God who restores balance to our lives. He is the one who brings our life into focus. We live with the promise of seeing God if we but hold out until the end. Our hearts live with the singular hope of one day seeing God and our loved ones face to face.

Blessed too the peacemakers. They shall be called children of God.

Blessed are we when we are instruments of peace. This beatitude helps us to remain peaceful as we sort through our memories, dreams, and reflections on our lives and the lives of those who have gone on before us as God's sons and daughters. The promise we hope in and live by is to receive the gift of that "peace which is beyond understanding."

Blessed are those persecuted for holiness' sake. The reign of God is theirs.

All around us is turmoil and chaos. We feel so hemmed in by our losses. The world is not compassionate and understanding. This too is a time for grace and salvation as we struggle with obstacles which try to block our acceptance of healing and salvation.

Blessed are you when they insult you and persecute you and utter every kind of slander against you because of me. Be glad and rejoice for your reward is great in heaven.

We must join our journey to the Lord's. How painful it

was for him and those who loved him. Think of his sorrowful mother and her pain in the face of such suffering. We look forward to being united at the table of the Lord in the Kingdom of Heaven "where every tear will be wiped away" and we will live peacefully in his Father's house where there are many mansions.

SECTION THREE

Continuing Our Journey

This section addresses the third phase of grieving. It is the period of readjustment. It usually lasts approximately three months. This follows the preceding six months of immediate loss and transition and may continue indefinitely. It is during this time that we realize the need for spiritual formation to continue our journey through life towards the Kingdom. Formation is not a once-and-for-all thing. Rather we need ongoing spiritual formation throughout our life. In this section we begin to ask questions which open new horizons for our faith.

Spiritual Transformation

How does the experience of loss affect our relationship with God?

It affects us in many ways. Some people, for example, come to have a better understanding about God, death, and eternal life.

When doubts arise how do we receive direction?

It is always better to work through our problems as a member of the Church. The believing community through prayerful support helps us to accept and find purpose during our bereavement. Just as St. Thomas the Apostle stayed with the community during his time of doubt, so too should we.

Is there pastoral help for the bereaved?

Along with parish support there are often other special programs which are offered. Retreats and seminars assist those who are mourning in a variety of ways. Many parishes list in their bulletins topics to be treated in their ongoing spiritual formation programs.

How can I receive help in identifying and coping with my feelings of loss?

Often those who are grieving complain that others are either insensitive or unwilling to listen to them. This happens in the grieving process when the phases of grief are not appreciated in our society. It seems that everyone has left us after the funeral and we find ourselves alone. This is the time to consider selecting a "loving listener."

Who is a "loving listener"?

A loving listener is a trusted friend who is willing to listen as we tell and retell our story of loss. Telling this story is very important for acceptance and healing during bereavement. Everyone's story is unique; each individual has special needs and concerns. The circumstances surrounding every loss color the way we grieve.

Who should be sought out as a loving listener?

A loving listener is someone (1) who is empathetic, (2) aware of what is involved in the grieving process, (3) sensitive to spiritual needs and beliefs, and (4) willing to make a commitment to be both supportive and present to you when you need them. There are similarities to this with the programs for addiction in which a person selects a sponsor. This individual assumes a very responsible role in a person's life.

During the time that we are trying to readjust and become reoriented in our lives how can talking with a loving listener make a difference?

The loving listener acts as a spiritual guide leading us out of confusion. That person in listening, reaffirms our worth and helps us cope with the indifference and insensitivity of society. He or she helps us to see the good in ourselves and in the world around us while we mourn.

What are some of the obstacles we need to recognize as we tell our story?

When we do not identify or recognize our anger it may

appear in a variety of ways. It may surface as sarcasm, apathy, depression, and even hostility.

What feelings often accompany our loss?

Anger is a frequent response to loss. We blame God and others for the pain we feel. Guilt, also, often surfaces. It may be authentic or misplaced guilt. We may need someone to help us correctly identify it. Guilt and anger can lead to isolation whether self-imposed or forced upon us by others. Mourning with deep-seated feelings of anger and guilt may lead us to withdraw from others in self-loathing.

Besides telling our story, how else can we communicate our loss?

Family prayers and rituals especially during the holiday seasons are very important since they acknowledge both our loss and our moving on.

Where in the Old Testament do we find an example of spiritual transformation through grief?

The Book of Job is an example of the spiritual changes which can occur while we mourn. In this book the puzzling issue of loss is confronted. In the first two chapters we find Job as a happy, well-balanced individual who has many blessings: children, good health, material well-being, and the respect of others. Job is kind and compassionate. In the third chapter he loses everything. His children are killed, his property is destroyed, his health is ruined and he is ostracized by others. His losses are unimaginable. And what does Job do? He remains steadfast in his faith in God. And in the end God rewards him a hundredfold for his patience and longsuffering.

Is there a lesson we can learn from Job?

Job never lost his faith or trust in God no matter how severely he was tried. His attitude in the face of misfortune and loss was unwavering: "'If we accept happiness from God's hand, must we not accept sorrow, too?' And in all his misfortune, Job uttered no sinful word" (Job 2:10).

What should we do when confronted with a loss?

St. Paul in his First Letter to the Thessalonians (5:17) tells us that we are to "never cease praying." In his Letter to the Ephesians (6:18) he also writes: "Pray at all times in the Spirit with every manner of prayer and supplication. Pray constantly and attentively for all in the holy company."

Prayer of the Church

What does the Church recommend as a way in which we can constantly pray?

The Church in the *Code of Canon Law* recommends that the Liturgy of the Hours, also known as the Divine Office or Breviary, become the prayer of the whole People of God (CCC, #1175).

What is the purpose of the Liturgy of the Hours?

The purpose of this liturgical way of praying is to offer at certain times during the day prayers which sanctify us and offer continual praise to God. Stopping several times during the day for brief prayer sets a rhythm that helps us keep focused on what is meaningful in our lives.

Are the prayers in the Liturgy of the Hours helpful for readjusting after a loss?

When we celebrate the Liturgy of the Hours especially in what is known as the "Office for the Dead" there is an acknowledging that "a spiritual bond links the Church on earth with the Church in heaven." When we pray for a loved one in this way we do so in union with the whole Church (OCF, #349). We are praying with our departed ones who are with the Lord. The Liturgy of the Hours helps us retain a spiritual focus at a time when it is most difficult.

How and when is the Office for the Dead prayed?

The Office is prayed in the morning and in the evening. It is an option for prayer at the Vigil for the deceased. It may be prayed at other times both privately and with others in community. Using the Office for the Dead places us in the eternal rhythm of the Church where the heavenly Kingdom and the earthly Church come together in praising God while acknowledging his love and the hope for eternal life with our deceased loved ones.

What are some of the healing aspects of the Liturgy of the Hours for those who mourn?

1. There is a new bond formed with our deceased loved one. Christ, who unites heaven and earth, helps us redefine this relationship.
2. When we assemble and pray the Office for the Dead, most notably the psalms, and we pray in the name of Christ, we unite our prayers to his in hope and love.
3. The psalms help us express our sorrow and our hope. Through them we acknowledge our suffering while reaffirming our faith. We know that there is more to life than what this world offers.

4. The psalms reaffirm us in the hope that our deceased loved one is participating in the life of heaven. We join with the psalmist as he is caught up in the joy of praising God and, in words written some three thousand years ago, we see clearly that there is more than the here and now.

Where are we able to find the Office for the Dead?

It is included in the *Order of Christian Funerals*, Part IV. It is also found in the Divine Office.

In the Office for the Dead there are two canticles or prayers. What significance do they have for us while we mourn?

The canticles are from Luke's Gospel. The first is Mary's *Magnificat* (Lk 1:46-55). This prayer reminds us of the wonderful ways of God. It places into perspective how God intervenes and brings us hope. In praying this canticle we are lifted up as Mary was through God's greatness. The second is a prophetic prayer by Zechariah, the father of John the Baptist. Again it is a hymn of hope trusting in the Lord's presence and action in our lives. In it, Zechariah proclaims how God will visit us in his mercy: "To shine on those who sit in darkness and in the shadow of death, and to guide our feet in the way of peace" (Lk 1:68-79).

Mary Our Model

How is Mary our model for mourning?

There are many titles given to Mary, among them "Our Lady of Sorrows," "Our Lady of Peace," "Our Lady of Consolation." These and many others were bestowed on her by generations of faithful who have sought her intercession especially during times of loss and stress.

How does devotion to Mary as our Mother of Sorrows give meaning to our loss?

We are reminded that Mary lost her husband Joseph. As a widow she suffered the loneliness of not having a loving partner with her as she continued her life's journey. She also is a mother who lost her child. This is a devastating occurrence for any parent. The Pietà beautifully expresses the intense sorrow of Mary as a parent. The steadfast faith and trust in God that she maintained in her own sorrow shows us how to accept and find meaning in our losses.

When did special devotion to Mary and her sorrows appear?

The faithful throughout the ages have always felt that Mary suffered much in the losses she experienced in her life. Particular devotion to the Sorrows of Mary appeared toward the beginning of the fourteenth century. This devotion was popularized by the Dominican Order. Initially five joys and five sorrows were enumerated. Eventually the joys and sorrows became seven. These correspond to the seven hours in the Office. These sorrows and joys were each meditated on during an hour of the day so we could better understand Mary and in so doing better appreciate how she epitomizes the model for the Christian life.

When did Mary, the mother of Jesus experience these seven sorrows?

1. When Jesus was arrested.
2. When Jesus was taken to Pilate for public judgment.
3. When the sentence of death was pronounced against Jesus.
4. When Mary saw Jesus nailed to a cross.

5. When Mary heard Jesus give up his spirit and die on the cross.
6. When Jesus' body was taken down from the cross.
7. When Jesus was wrapped in linen and laid in the tomb.

Each of these sorrows was like a dagger to Mary's heart. Just as our memories stab us so too did Mary suffer in her sorrows. Her example shows us how we, too, can cope with our losses.

How is this devotion practiced in our own time?

There have been some changes through time in the enumeration of the seven sorrows. The present form includes the losses Mary experienced even during Jesus' childhood. These sorrows are a source for healing and hope when they are meditated on by those who mourn.

How do we understand the seven sorrows of Mary in our own day?

All of the following seven sorrows have scriptural roots which serve as healing meditations as we grieve.

1. The Prophecy of Simeon (Lk 2:34-35)

"Simeon blessed them and said to Mary his mother: 'This child is destined to be the downfall and the rise of many in Israel, a sign that will be opposed—and you yourself shall be pierced with a sword—so that the thoughts of many hearts may be laid bare.'" The first sorrow is fear—fear of losing our loved one, especially as an infant. Mary shows us that while fear hovers over us we cannot let it paralyze us and our love of life. She simply offers it up and goes on with her life. She does not allow fear to stifle her steadfast love.

2. The Flight into Egypt (Mt 2:13-21)

This passage recounts the story of the Holy Family experiencing the crisis of having to flee persecution from Herod. It illustrates the turmoil and displacement which occurred for Mary and Joseph as they tried to protect their infant son. Here we see more fear, this time immediate. Mary once again acts in concert with Joseph to protect the family and put it in a place where it can be safe and develop.

3. The Loss of Jesus for Three Days in the Temple (Lk 2:41-50)

This is a story from Jesus' early years. Jesus' separation from his parents caused Mary and Joseph unimaginable anxiety. A lost child is every parent's nightmare. This sorrow had to greatly affect Mary. Mary knew her son was different and special. She didn't try to change him yet she did fear for him as every mother does when something like this happens. She put her trust in God to protect her child.

4. The Ascent to Calvary (Jn 19:17)

When we see a loved one suffering there is considerable pain. Mary had to witness Jesus being so unjustly treated. Just to look upon his face and body and see his pain became her pain. Here, the fears Mary has learned to cope with became almost overwhelming. Still the worst was yet to come. In silence and at a distance, she lends her love and strength to Jesus in his time of trial.

5. The Crucifixion and Death of Jesus (Jn 19:18-30)

It is agonizingly difficult to be with a loved one when they die. Mary saw Jesus give up his spirit. She suffered with her son until the very end. As is so often the case in the death of a loved one we feel that part of ourselves has died as well. Mary experienced this intense loss. The worst has happened. A mother was left behind to bury her son. The sword that Simeon spoke of has been driven deep into her heart. Perhaps Mary gained strength from recalling the words of the Angel Gabriel and his promises to her.

6. Jesus is Taken Down from the Cross (Jn 19:39-40)

There are moments of intense sorrow surrounding the death of a loved one. When we first gather together at a time of death there is unspeakable sadness. The picture of Jesus' body in his mother's arms is the picture of grief for our faith. This image remains with us as a symbol of our loss and faith. With Mary, we know this is not the end.

7. Jesus is Laid in the Tomb (Jn 19:40-42)

Mary had to suffer the burial of her son's body. She too had to separate herself from his physical presence and to readjust her life without her only son. Mary busies herself and, for the last time, performs this final act of love for her son. She knows this loss will end.

How is Mary's "Way of the Cross" a model for our mourning?

A traditional Latin hymn for the "Way of the Cross" entitled *Stabat Mater* ("the mother was standing") describes in twenty couplets the sorrow of Mary as she stood beneath the cross and participated in her son's sacrifice for our salvation.

Which stations show Mary's suffering with Jesus?

The Fourth Station: "Jesus Meets His Mother" expresses the deep sorrow Mary must have felt. It is along the way that Jesus meets his mother who is filled with grief. How deep is her pain as she sees her son suffering.

What is the lesson for us from this station concerning our own grief?

Like Mary we agonize when our loved ones suffer. Their pain becomes our own. This shared pain becomes an ache in our hearts. We see in Mary her compassion and love and we ask her to assist us while we mourn. Mary can relate to our loss and she offers to be with us in our time of need.

How does the Thirteenth Station help us in our grief?

The Thirteenth Station: "Jesus is Taken Down from the Cross" reminds us of Mary as she, in the company of the apostle John and a few other friends, carefully removed the body of Jesus from the cross. Mary briefly held her only son in her arms. She was aware that she held the one who alone brings true life and shows the way to the Father. Even in her grief she saw beyond her own sorrow to her conviction that the darkness of this moment would give way to the light of her son's resurrection.

How does the "Way of the Cross" help us while we grieve?

When we pray the "Way of the Cross" we acknowledge our pain and suffering and join it to the Lord's. We ask Jesus and his mother to help us see beyond our grief to the resurrection.

What is the most popular devotion to Mary?

The Rosary is the most popular devotion to Mary. By meditating on the mysteries we find peace especially while we mourn. The complete Rosary consists of fifteen decades. Normally, five decades are recited at a time.

Through the repetition of the Hail Mary's we are able to focus our attention on the mystery. This is very helpful because, while we grieve there are so many distractions. We need to focus our hearts and lives on God during the difficult time of bereavement.

The Joyful, Sorrowful and Glorious Mysteries of the Rosary

The Joyful Mysteries
1. The Annunciation: *This mystery speaks to our acceptance of God's intervention in our lives. Lord, help me to meditate on your will for me in this situation and what it means in the light of eternity.*
2. The Visitation of Mary to Elizabeth: *Lord, help me to accept graciously those who visit to bring me love and support. Help me to realize how others can be an instrument of your compassion and love for me at this time.*
3. The Birth of Jesus: *Help me to think of the death of my loved one as a birth to eternal life.*
4. The Presentation of Jesus in the Temple: *O Lord, help me to realize that our lives are lived in the sacredness of your presence. I ask you to bring my loved one into your presence in the Kingdom of Heaven.*
5. The Finding of Jesus in the Temple: *Lord, so often I feel lost. I ask you to give me the joy of realizing that I am not alone and that you always find me even though I hide in my sorrow. Send me that joy of being one with you.*

The Sorrowful Mysteries
1. The Agony in the Garden: *In my sorrow I need to be one with you as I experience the agony of this loss. You*

are with me helping me to accept what is so very pain-
ful. Not my will but yours be done.

2. The Scourging at the Pillar: *My entire body is weak*
   from my mourning. I feel as if I am being scourged by
   sorrow. Let me offer this up as you did for the love of
   others especially my loved one.

3. The Crowning with Thorns: *What grief you must have*
   felt as your sacred head was bruised and cut from the
   thorns. My head feels as if I cannot bear the burden of
   this grief. Help me to stand at the foot of the cross and
   be healed of my hurts because of your love.

4. The Carrying of the Cross: *My grief is to carry this cross*
   which I reluctantly take up. You, who shouldered your
   cross for me, are my strength. Help me to bear this cross
   as I cry out to you.

5. The Crucifixion: *Lord, as I stand at the foot of the cross*
   I cry out in the anguish of so much loss. Increase my
   trust and love for you who promised so much to those
   who follow you. Help me to see beyond my own blind-
   ness and to walk by faith.

The Glorious Mysteries

1. The Resurrection: *The Father raised you up in glory. I*
   want to share in a similar resurrection to yours with all
   of those whom I love. Help me to see life through this
   mystery which gives meaning to my mourning.

2. The Ascension: *We did not lose you, Lord Jesus, in*
   your return to the Father. So too I need to believe that I
   have not lost my loved ones born to eternal life. I look
   forward to being with you and them in the Kingdom of
   Heaven according to your will and in your good time.

3. The Descent of the Holy Spirit Upon the Apostles: *I*
   ask you, Lord, to send your Holy Spirit given to me at

Baptism to me as I seek your glorification of my loved one. You alone are Lord, to you alone do I give glory and praise forever.

4. The Assumption of Mary into Heaven: *Through the intercession of Mary I pray for the life of heaven for myself and all of those dear to me. Your love, O Mary, is a love which brings healing from the sorrows so seated in your heart. Only your son can bring about lasting glory.*

5. The Crowning of Mary Queen of Heaven: *How wonderful is the eternal life of heaven. I look forward to the wonderful things God has prepared. Your love, O Mary, and your presence in the Kingdom brings me great joy and consolation.*

Society and the Bereaved

What must our society do for the bereaved to ensure that they have the time they need to mourn?

Our society has to cooperate in helping the bereaved to readjust their lives. There are basic rights which the bereaved ought to have in our communities.

Is it necessary to spell out a bill of rights for the bereaved?

Our earliest history lessons taught us the importance of having a bill of rights. The lessons emphasized that there was a need for a summary of the fundamental rights and privileges guaranteed to a people against violations by society.

What Are the Basic Rights of Those Who Mourn?

1. The bereaved have the right to express themselves. *This right is necessary for anyone undergoing a loss.*

Not to encourage the bereaved to express their sense of emptiness, their feelings of abandonment, searching, guilt, and other common symptoms characteristic of loss only inhibits and hurts their spiritual, psychological, and physical well-being.

2. The bereaved have the right to grieve and receive permission from others to grieve. *Far too often society ignores either the bereaved or their feelings. This is especially evident in the work force where "bereavement time" is not sufficient or does not exist.*

3. Right to connect with others, especially through support groups, grief seminars, and retreats. *Isolation or withdrawal from others inhibits good grief work. There are tasks facing the bereaved which must be fulfilled. These range from emotional acceptance to assistance in making necessary economic and social changes. People not only have a right to express themselves and expect respect but also they need avenues for this expression.*

4. Right to confidentiality. *The circumstances surrounding a loss are not always something that the bereaved want to share. They have the right to protect the memory of their loved ones. Very often prying questions are put to the bereaved. This is not a sensitive or confidential way of relating. Support groups have to be particularly sensitive to the confidentiality of the participants. Very often this has to be spelled out in the ground rules for times when they meet. The fact of grief should be enough of a catalyst to reach out to the bereaved. We do not need information about the deceased beyond what is offered.*

5. Right to tell the story of loss. *In order to accept a loss it is often necessary for the bereaved to tell and retell their story. They should be allowed to do this without*

being cut off or discouraged. It is healing for the bereaved to do this as the acceptance of the reality of their loss is helped by openly recalling the loss.

6. Right to develop a new spiritual relationship with the deceased. *Living in a secular society is difficult for the bereaved. Religious sensitivity is not always a value. Unfortunately religious practices are not always encouraged even in extended families. I can recall an aged person who could not receive help from family members to have a date set for a memorial Mass. Family participation in helping others find meaning amidst chaos is not always forthcoming. Parish bereavement committees have to be aware of secular forces which are not there to assist those who mourn in spiritual matters. Rather than wait, parish bereavement ministers should take the initiative and invite family participation and memorializing.*

7. The bereaved have the right to be treated fairly especially during times of loss. *It is not uncommon for those who are suffering a loss to be taken advantage of during an emotional upheaval. Stories abound about violations of consumer rights during funerals and divorces. People do not have options clearly explained. Very often procedures at alarming cost are already put into place before the bereaved are provided adequate information. Such practices have to be continually addressed by good legislation and enforcement. Bereavement committees in parishes can help alleviate this abuse by providing informational resources to people on a regular basis not just at the time of grief.*

8. Right to be treated in a normal way by others. *Grief is a natural occurrence in all of our lives. It is not an ill-*

ness. To experience loss is just as human as the experience of birth, marriage, and other events in the course of our lifetime. Those who are mourning do not become fragile vessels to be put away from harm. Physicians should be especially sensitive to what is normal and not be too quick to skirt the process through medications that are more often prescribed due to misled family members' concerns than the real needs of the bereaved.

9. Right to self-esteem. *When a significant loss occurs the bereaved may have considerable difficulty with self-image. So very often society defines others by their relationships or what a person does. Self-worth is affected while we grieve. It is important to remember that the loss of a loved one, a position, or a relationship does not make us less lovable. While our lifestyle might change or be affected by loss, we remain as we are, creatures of God entitled to respect and love.*

10. The bereaved have the right to remember and ritualize the loss. *Far too often there is a conspiracy of silence surrounding our losses. Society does not make mention of loss. Everyone experiences public and private losses. When we realize that this is part of our journey then our limitations are more easily accepted. Bereaved relatives are too often not being allowed to grieve at funerals or remember in ritualized ways the loss of a loved one in death. The funeral arrangements are placed in the hands of administrators of estates. The option to quickly bury the person is made without other family members, let alone the deceased loved one's wishes being adhered to. It has been suggested that proxies for funerals similar to health care proxies be developed. Such proxies would go far to respect the deceased's and their family's wishes.*

SECTION FOUR

Afterword

It is necessary that some final words accompany this work. When we pick up a book to help us especially during critical moments we may be swept up in the "self-help" approach. The following words are meant to highlight what we should understand about such help and put it into perspective. It has been the intent of this work to place our loss into the context of spirituality. This section of the book is meant to assist us in better ways to appreciate how spiritual help is given.

Bookstores are filled with self-help publications. Everyone is interested in "how to" approaches for improving their lives. Secular programs emphasize self-reliance. Unfortunately certain methods and techniques fall short in addressing the whole person. There has to be a spiritual component for real improvement. Not to see the whole context for whatever ventures we have in life will only make our efforts devoid of real and lasting purpose. The challenge facing us is how well we can connect self-help programs to spirituality in our lives.

Spiritual Context

A spirituality for self-help does not focus solely on self-reliance. Rather the spiritual approach allows us to emphasize the importance of surrendering one's self. No matter what the program or concern, there is a need to let go of life's attachments which so often control a person. It stands to reason that control issues are better resolved when we learn how to become detached. This leads the way for better handling what before was unmanageable.

When we rely on ourselves alone the outcome is not religious. Self-absorption does not allow us to see that we need to transcend ourselves in order to make a lasting change in our lives. This transformation happens when we follow certain rules. We may improve somewhat with a diet or a relaxation response, but how that nurtures our spirit is the ultimate test. Very often people who are able to overcome smoking remark that what happened in their lives changed them for the better. Many state that the smoke cessation program brought them to a better appreciation of spirituality in their lives. They realized in a better way that they are images of God and must take care of their bodies. Others have remarked that they never realized what the meaning of free will was until this compulsion was overcome.

We are able to change when we call upon the deep resources of faith. Our habits, addictions, and compulsions have to be dealt with in the broader contexts of life, including the spiritual dimension. If we limit our view to this world only and the physical dimension we miss out on the broader picture.

A Misinterpretation

A celebrity on a recent late night talk show on TV was telling how she kept herself looking young through a self-help technique. In the course of the interview she continually stressed personal strength and self-reliance. The most telling remark of the interview was when she said: "I have all I can do just to keep my heart beating."

This, of course, is utter nonsense. None of us is able to "will" our hearts into beating. In spiritual terms we believe that in *God* we "live and breathe and have our being."

Self-Reliance and Self-Transcendence

Each of us has been given by God an inner source of strength and power. Developing this inner power requires spiritual exercise. The Spiritual Exercises of St. Ignatius Loyola are used frequently in retreat programs and are familiar to many because of their structure. But there are others that are just as well-known, among the best of which are the step programs which explicitly stress spirituality. The most familiar among the steps programs is the one for Alcoholics Anonymous. *Twelve Steps and Twelve Traditions* is a spiritual program. Many other step programs have spun off from A.A.'s Twelve Step Program. These deal with overeating, drug abuse, and other addictions. The Twelve Steps are also helpful as a spiritual structure for those experiencing life's losses. My own work *Six Steps for Managing Loss: A Catholic Guide Through Grief* has for its focus how a step program relates to grief.

Admitting Our Powerlessness

Personal empowerment is necessary for self-help. Strange as it may seem, real empowerment is given to us as human beings when we realize our limitations. A spiritual self-help program depends upon the admission that we are powerless, that on our own we could not resolve our conflicts, handle our compulsions or deal with our loss. The admission of our personal emptiness is the very foundation for all of the steps we take toward wellness and wholeness.

The realization that we are finite enables us to see ourselves in an honest way. Real change in the form of personal transformation only seems to begin when we admit our powerlessness. This opens us up to become connected to the real source of power.

Out of the Depths

The faith of the psalmist in Psalm 130, "Out of the Depths," touches many feelings all of us have when we are in need of help. The psalm gives voice to our own inability to lift ourselves up in body, mind, and spirit. We need to realize that whatever we do is accomplished not by ourselves alone but only through our relationship with God. The real meaning of our justification depends upon God's love which makes everything possible.

In our self-help programs we tend to become very task oriented. We want to make things happen. It is important not to allow the process to consume us. We must listen to the psalmist: "I trust in the Lord; my soul waits for the Lord more than sentinels wait for the dawn."

Higher Power

Belief in a Higher Power who is present, able and willing to help us, gives us the courage and strength we need to live out our lives in growth-filled ways. Reliance upon the Creator enables us to respond creatively to life's problems, including the loss of a loved one. Our personal relationship with God is what is needed to experience that intimacy which is so very necessary to us in such a time.

We need to connect with the source of all strength, consolation, and hope. Whatever techniques we employ are merely vehicles for the much greater transformations which affect our spirit. It is little wonder that the first spiritual directors for people seeking healing and forgiveness were called "soul directors."

Conforming Our Will

Most of us are familiar with the phrase "Let go and let God." These words tell us not to insist on doing it all on our own (which admittedly we cannot) but to leave that which we cannot change in the hands of God. Often that means accepting the will of God. When we battle or reject God's will we are trying to take charge of our own lives when we lack the resources to do so. We cannot live as our own master. Real spiritual growth occurs when we topple the idols in our lives. The highest form of pride is that which makes us out to be the Creator rather than the creature. When our wills dominate and we try to place God over to the side, then whatever we do will not really be helpful and might even harm.

Spiritual Inventory

In every kind of program we need to assess how we are doing. The way we assess often depends upon the questions we raise. If our focus is exclusively on the physical changes that we note in ourselves as we come to terms with our grief, then we have overlooked the spiritual changes. A spiritual inventory requires courage to look at our relationships and realistically assess whether we need to bring healing and forgiveness into them. This is an essential spiritual reality for every spiritual self-help program.

Our assessment must also look at how well we are doing in turning over and surrendering our lives to God. How well we have abandoned ourselves to God and his will is at the core of spiritual theology. All of the mystical saints have shown us down through the ages a variety of ways to accomplish this.

Journaling and Self-Help

God speaks to us in a variety of ways. For many the idea of keeping a journal indicating how they are doing as they work through their grief is highly meaningful. The journal is also a very useful instrument for gaining spiritual insights. In many ways as we trust and surrender to the Lord we are amazed at the new ideas and insights that we are given. Where do such thoughts originate? This is just one of the miracles of God's continual self-revelation.

Concluding Self-Help and Spirituality Points

1. Always keep in mind that we are spiritual beings and whatever we do has spiritual ramifications.
2. See the relationship between self-help programs and a spiritual approach to life.
3. Assess how well you are doing in terms of spiritual growth through a spiritual inventory or journal.
4. Realize that the goal is always a better relationship with God through surrender to his will.

If we keep some of these points in mind when we consider self-help programs we can really benefit in many more ways. It is essential that we place what we are doing in the broader context of faith. Our trust in God only increases when we do the best we can as those created in his image to enhance that image with God's help.

SECTION FIVE

Appendices

Appendix A

Remembering in Faith

The way we remember a loved one who has died plays a central role and considerably influences how well we grieve. One of the primary tasks for good grief work is to form a new relationship with someone now separated from us by death.

When we hear that someone we know has died they are more in our minds than at any other time. The news of a death floods our consciousness with thoughts about our loved one which we thought were long ago forgotten. We may recall incidents that took place a long, long time ago as if they had recently occurred. Characteristics such as mannerisms that we never really focused on when they were alive are far more vivid to us as we recall our deceased loved one. The following pastoral example illustrates the role of remembering.

> Marian had moved out of state approximately six years ago. She kept in contact with family members as best she could. A phone call came telling her of Aunt Helen's death. Immediately Marian recalled visiting her aunt and making apple pies with her. In her grief she could relive what it was like to sift the flour and roll the dough.

For Marian this was a vivid memory of her Aunt which went back to her own childhood. There are many memories we have of loved ones. Yet it seems that what will touch us at moments of loss are thoughts and remembrances which we hardly ever considered.

A Graced Time

Most of us never think about grief as a time for growth. Early on in our bereavement we feel nearly devastated by our emotions. Sometimes the only real consolation we have is in knowing that things will not be this way forever. Then gradually the initial phase of numbness and shock gives way to a time of transition. This period can be equally if not more painful for us. Up to then our emotions were pretty well anesthetized by the trauma of the situation. Now we must really face and accept our loss. The amount of time this will take depends upon the degree of our affectional tie with the loved one. This varies according to the uniqueness of our personalities and how well or poorly we have handled loss in the past.

During these months of transition we can experience spiritual changes in our lives. Our faith instructs us that there is light in the darkness. As Christians we need to call upon the rich resources of faith. Many signs, symbols, rituals, images, and ways of meditating relate to our loss. Utilizing these resources can convert our grief into grace. We can make some sense out of the chaos and confusion and find meaning in our lives.

During bereavement we experience certain symptoms. There are many spiritual realities which speak to these symptoms. For example, a feeling of abandonment is a significant reality that we may have to deal with in our grief. We may feel abandoned by the loved one who has died, by our friends, and even by God. If we can convert these feelings into new ways of letting go and abandoning ourselves to God, we experience the grace of healing.

Sorting Out

It is no easy task to sort things out while we grieve. When there is intense grief we can easily become disoriented. Very often the bereaved question the state of their mental health in all the chaos. It is psychologically sound to become confused and disoriented in this situation. This is a normal response to loss. We do not have to seek professional help in our confusion, but we should seek out others who are compassionate and willing to listen to our story of loss. It is a story that must be told and retold. The more we tell it the more we begin to sort things out. Our story told to a compassionate listener helps us to accept the reality of loss. We recall those memories which loom larger than life about our time with the deceased. We begin to determine what we want to hold onto and what we must let go of.

Remembering in Scripture

Recalling and narrating God's actions in Scripture are ways of "remembering" (meaning "to make present"). God is made present to us when we hear his word proclaimed in the Bible. There is always an eternal dimension to our recalling the images and events recorded there. In the Hebrew mentality recalling the past makes it a present reality.

The role of remembrance in the Psalms illustrates the significance of remembrance. The psalmist says: "My soul is cast down within me, therefore I remember you" (Ps 42:6) Memory revives faith. In the Scriptures there is the twofold aspect of the great acts of remembering. God remembers and we remember. Even though we are lamenting a loss there is always that remembrance that God has not forgotten his covenant with us: "For their sake he remembered his covenant, and showed compassion according to his steadfast love" (Ps 106:45).

Covenantal Love

In the *Order of Christian Funerals* during the final commendation and farewell mention is made of the fact that the ties of friendship which bind us together in life do not cease in death. This is an aspect of covenantal love, the kind of love that endures beyond the grave. Remembering our loved ones has to be placed in this context as we develop a new and deeply spiritual relationship with them.

Recollections

During the funeral rites, family members often read a remembrance about the deceased loved one. Since the promulgation of the new funeral ritual in 1989 there has been some debate as to the most appropriate time for this to happen. At this time most parishes include it during the final farewell. At the same time, pastors are finding that there is a need for more instruction or catechesis about what this type of remembrance really means.

Remembering in the form of a eulogy does not normally relate the life of a loved one in the context of faith. What is frequently lacking is the realization that all that we accomplish in life is really given to us by our loving God. After all, we only live and move and have our being because God constantly remembers us. Eulogies that forget or ignore this faith dimension limit our understanding of the grace given all of us to do what we do in life. We cannot attribute human deeds to our initiative alone.

Remembering in the future may be better placed during the time of the Vigil. The Vigil appears to be a more suitable time to look at the journey and those who have died as it relates to watching and waiting for the Lord's return in glory. There can be a suitable remembrance when we place what has happened in our lives into the context of how well we lived in the presence of God. When we examine the life of a Christian in death we are able to look back over the entire journey. Up until that point it is impossible to ascertain an overall pattern.

During the Vigil we hear the prayer that for the Christian only "your good works go with you." This is a wonderful way of celebrating the meaning of a Christian's life lived out in faith and good works.

St. Paul illustrates what it means to know that it is God who acts in our lives. If we want to really gain insight to the Catholic tradition of avoiding eulogies we can find that basis in Scripture by exploring Paul's writings. A remarkable insight to what we are able to accomplish because God strengthens us is found in his Second Letter to the Corinthians (1:3-7): "Let us give thanks to the God and Father of our Lord Jesus Christ, the compassionate Father, the God from whom all help comes! He helps us in all of our afflictions, so that we will be able to help others who have all kinds of troubles, using the same help that we ourselves have received from God."

Paul explains in his letters that we really cannot do anything worthwhile on our own. As we remember those who have died it is essential that we appreciate their good works in this context.

Remembering in Faith

Our memories are not meant for torturing us. They certainly do elicit emotions. When avoidance is practiced we block the necessary healing. How we remember is essential. Ways to resolve our loss and accept it depend upon how well we explore the spiritual dimensions. Secular society ignores the deep significance of spiritual bonding. Our society does not help us to transcend and to appreciate the ultimate purpose of life. This was emphasized in Pope John Paul II's encyclical *Reason and Faith.*

Grief ministry can suffer from over psychologizing loss and ways to treat it and not paying enough attention to the spiritual dimension. It can get caught up in the jargon of grief and fail to address people's spiritual needs. This must be avoided in our workshops, support groups and most especially in liturgical expression.

Times to Remember

Throughout the entire liturgical cycle there are times for us to remember all those who have died.

During Advent we look forward to the Lord's coming again in glory. This waiting is very characteristic of bereavement. The Christmas season is a very difficult time for those suffering loss. During Advent many parishes find that support groups and special liturgies are especially helpful for the bereaved.

The Lenten season is another time when we receive special grace in our remembrance as we await the celebration of Easter. The journey from ashes to Easter is so similar to the way we go through grief. While we grieve we often anxiously yearn for our loved one's presence. So too our Lenten journey is a time when we yearn for the celebration of the Lord's resurrectional presence.

How well we do in placing our memories into the context of faith directly affects meaning in our lives. Purposeful remembering is only accomplished when we do not lose sight of the bright promise of immortality. Our recalling is then a looking forward to the time when we will all be together with those whom we continue to love in the Spirit.

Remembering and Petitioning for Help

We need assistance in living with our memories. The Memorare is a prayer of devotion seeking Mary's help. The word "memorare" means "to remember" in Latin. Our devotion to Mary and this prayer is very helpful to us while we grieve.

The Memorare

Remember, O most gracious Virgin Mary,
    that never was it known
    that anyone who fled to your protection,
    implored your help,
    or sought your intercession,
        was left unaided.
    Inspired by this confidence,
        I fly unto you, O Virgin of Virgins, my
Mother;
To you do I come,
    before you I stand, sinful and sorrowful.
O Mother of the Word Incarnate,
    despise not my petitions,
    but in your mercy, hear and answer me. Amen.

Appendix B

The Seven Last Words

Traditionally the words of Jesus from the cross have always been a source of strength and consolation for Christians. Down through the ages the story of Jesus' life, death, and resurrection has been told and retold. The eternal aspects of this saving action continually give new strength to all of us who are in need of healing and hope.

The story of Jesus' life, death, and resurrection is truly the greatest story ever told. Our life story only finds meaning when we can relate it to Jesus. We have to see our lives through the eyes of faith and realize that we are meant one day to be with the Lord for all eternity. When we can meditate on the full significance of these words healing occurs.

The spiritual, emotional, and physical healing all of us need to continue our journey has been given to us by Jesus in his redemptive act of suffering on the cross for us once and for all. We pray that we will have eyes to see and ears to hear what this means for us, especially during critical moments in our life's journey.

Meditation is a way for us as Christians to ponder the mysteries of our existence. We begin by placing ourselves at the foot of the cross. Our souls need to hear the final words of

Jesus to us as we struggle to accept the cross and continue to live out our lives graced by what he has done for us. Our conversation with the Lord on the cross brings not only new hope but also conversion. We hand over to him our feelings of anger, emptiness, guilt, yearning, and anxiety and promise, with his grace, to live a changed life. We may call upon the name of the Lord and ask that our crosses be lightened knowing that Jesus took our sins and suffering on himself out of love for us.

The Traditional Devotion to the Seven Last Words

The Seven Last Words are an expression of a devotional tradition among many in the Church. Communities of faith for centuries have meditated on these words and found inspiration for their lives.

The number seven in Sacred Scripture symbolizes fullness or completeness. We recall the seven days for creation, the seven diadems in the Book of Revelation, the seven gifts of the Holy Spirit, the seven sacraments, all of which point to fulfillment.

Life Over Death

The Seven Last Words give us a deep insight into the spirituality of the Cross. With us even to the very end of his earthly life, Jesus is completing on the Cross the work his Father had sent him to do. The purpose behind everything that Jesus did was to give us life, a new and more abundant life. We realize in the living words of this devotion not only Jesus' unconditional love for us but how unselfishly he accepted even to die for us.

Our Christian life must conform to Jesus' life, death, and resurrection. Through our own crosses we can experience how our journey only takes on meaning in light of the Cross of Jesus.

The Seven Last Words According to Sacred Scripture

The First Word (Luke 23:34): "Father, forgive them for they know not what they do."
The Second Word (Luke 23:43): "Amen, amen, I say to you, today you will be with me in Paradise."
The Third Word (John 19:26-27): "He said to his mother, 'Woman, behold, your son.' Then he said to his disciple, 'Behold your mother.'"
The Fourth Word (Matthew 27:46; Mark 15:34): "My God, my God, why have you forsaken me?"
The Fifth Word (John 19:28): "I thirst."
The Sixth Word (John 19:30): "It is finished."
The Seventh Word (Luke 23:46): "Father, into your hands I commend my spirit."

The word of God forms the believing community. When we hear the word we experience the healing presence of the Holy Spirit. As hearers of the word we want to explore ways to relate revelation to our needs as we journey. Our loneliness, emptiness, feelings of abandonment, searching and longing for fulfillment and many other emotions all cry out for purpose. These words speak to the broken-hearted as well as to those who are compassionate healers. All of us very often find ourselves in either place at various times during our lives.

Dying, death, and bereavement are in our present day's consciousness perhaps more than in the past. Along with this new awareness is the need to relate these realities to faith.

Community Prayer

It is only fitting that a spiritual work of this nature take place in a community of faith. In many ways what we struggle with in our lives is what defines who we are in the context of faith. We may want to write about our journey and how it relates to these last words.

Paradoxically, what has been in our traditional devotion called "last" becomes "first" once again as these words help us sort out our emotional and spiritual responses to life itself.

Glossary of Terms for Grief

abandonment: a feeling of being left alone, rejected, unsupported, lost and bereft of help. It is an emotion often felt while grieving and is particularly associated with the death of someone very close such as a parent, spouse, or other close associate.

acceptance: the process of willingly embracing something or someone. When applied to grief, it refers to the willing embrace of our loss. Avoidance only complicates our bereavement and then other difficulties often surface. In the process of bereavement, there is an initial acceptance that something has really occurred. After the numbness and shock have worn off, there is a further coming to acknowledge that we have truly accepted the event. This is often described as the acceptance of acceptance.

affectional ties: emotional bonds of affection which vary according to the degree of intimacy and love. The severing of an affectional tie or bond creates a crisis that cries out for expression. The severing of a loved one from ourselves in death is as if part of ourselves has succumbed as well. We need to go through a grieving process when such a separation occurs.

anniversary affect: the emotions triggered by the celebration of an anniversary. This does not mean returning to square one in our grief. The bereaved often fear that the celebration of the anniversary will be so devastating that they will have to go back and start all over again. It is rather the confirmation of the fact that there is really no time limit for our grief. Anniversaries need to be ritualized. It is important to celebrate the memory of loved ones at special times.

anticipatory grief: the fear and sadness felt before the actual death of a loved one. Anticipating a loss may be as devastating for some as the loss itself. When someone is dying the anticipatory grief can be intense. It builds up to the event. This kind of grief is for all concerned an anxiety-provoking experience in our lives.

bereavement: this is the time spent in mourning. There is no set time for bereavement. Society does not allow people enough time to grieve. The phases of grief may take about a year. However, the actual loss may be with us for a lifetime. Anniversaries and other memorable events bear this out as true.

catechism: a short book giving, in question-and-answer form, a brief summary of the basic principles of a religion. Jesus' Sermon on the Mount is an example of his fundamental teachings or catechesis. The goal of a catechism is to teach and form the religious conscience of its readers and bring them closer to the Lord.

catharsis: a purifying or figurative cleansing or release of the emotions. Crying during bereavement can be a cathartic experience. The tears, as an expression of our feelings of great loss, provide a kind of cleansing and release of our emotions. Cathartic experiences are encouraged and not to be shunned. Crying is encouraged as a way of coming to terms with our grief and eventual acceptance of our loss.

cemetery: the place of burial. The Catholic cemetery is consecrated ground that has already been blessed. Secular cemeteries receive a blessing at the time of burial.

chaos: the condition of total disorder or confusion. The experience of grief has often been described as chaotic. Our entire world view has been shaken and we need to make some sense of what is going on around us. It can be very disorienting and confusing. Everything seems to have changed and we want to be able to give some shape to the disorder in our lives.

committal: the act of entrusting the body of the deceased to its final resting place. Prayers are offered at the cemetery when the Christian's body or cremains are committed to the earth. These prayers are also offered when there is burial at sea.

compassionate listener: a person who is willing to lend a sympathetic ear during a time of crisis. This may be a trusted friend or relative who is empathetic, patient and understanding. They must be willing to accompany you as you embark on this journey through darkness to light.

complicated grief: grief coupled with depression. For the most part grief is not a mental health emergency. It is a perfectly normal experience, a part of being human. As life begins at birth so it ends in death for everyone.

cremation: the incineration of a corpse. It is a form of disposing of the human body allowed by most mainline religions. In the Catholic Church there are requirements for the presence of the cremains at the funeral and the disposition of the cremains. They must be buried in the ground. In 1997 the *Order of Christian Funerals* published an appendix to be used in funeral rites in the presence of cremated remains. Cremation is a growing custom in the United States.

crisis: a crucial or decisive point or situation; a turning point in life. Loss is a crisis that triggers stressors which must be addressed. It throws our lives into a turmoil as the event brings about an immediate and irreversible change from the way things were. In order to process what is happening we very often need help. We cannot always sort things out by ourselves.

denial: a refusal to accept the truth of a situation. Very often those experiencing loss practice denial to avoid facing what has really happened. Sometimes the denial is so pronounced that the individual will not even allow another to mention the loss in his or her presence. Extreme cases include a loss of contact with reality in other areas as well.

detachment: indifference to worldly affairs or the concerns of others; the act of separating ourselves from that to which we were once closely associated. It is necessary to detach ourselves from the person who is the object of our loss. The physical presence has to give way to memory. Letting go and beginning to develop a new spiritual relationship with the loved one who has died is part of the process. The inability to let go may be a control issue for the bereaved. Sometimes there is a feeling of guilt in letting go, falsely assuming that such is an expression of not loving the deceased.

distractibility: having one's attention diverted from its original focus during a time of extreme mental or emotional disturbance. Mild distractibility may occur while grieving. We may not be aware of what we are doing due to our mind's preoccupation with the loss. This is normal and yet something we have to be aware of especially while driving a car or performing other activities requiring our undivided attention.

emptiness: devoid of purpose; a sense that everything is meaningless. Life seems to be lacking in energy. Physically we may feel that there is a great void. Our souls cry out for some kind of purpose to fill our sense of loss. This emptiness is like a dark night for our senses.

eulogy: a laudatory speech of praise and commendation frequently given at the time of a funeral. Eulogies extol the worldly accomplishments of the deceased generally without reference to the spiritual motivation behind them. Such eulogies are not offered within the ritual moments of a Catholic funeral. The sacred approach to speaking of the deceased extols God's gifts allowing him or her to achieve in life.

farewell: words addressed at the time of parting. It has become a practice for a family member or friend to offer farewell remarks during the Final Commendation and Farewell of the Funeral Mass. It is meant to be a remembrance in the context of faith.

funeral: the ceremonies held in connection with the burial or cremation of the dead. The funeral is the first public expression of mourning. It is the dignified manner in which loved ones remember the deceased in the context of faith. The rites vary according to religious beliefs. There are definite rituals or stations which occur in Catholic funeral rites. Funerals provide us with an opportunity to remember the deceased and to bring comfort to the living. How much we care for one another is often reflected in how we participate in these rites.

funeral homily: the sermon given in the context of a Funeral Mass. It communicates the faith of the believing community as we confront death and conveys the hope we have in the resurrection of the dead. As such it brings much needed consolation to the bereaved.

Funeral Mass: the Roman Catholic celebration of the suffering, death and resurrection of Christ. Usually the rite of Christian funerals is celebrated within the Funeral Mass. It reminds us of our oneness with Jesus' paschal mystery.

grief: the deep mental anguish and sorrow which accompanies the awareness of a loss. This recognition is intensely personal and is very much involved in the subjective perception as to who or what is lost. Grief manifests itself in many different ways and may profoundly affect the behavior of the one suffering the separation and loss.

high grief / low grief: the intensity of our grief depends on how strong or weak our ties are to the deceased. High grief usually describes a very intense love relationship (the death of a parent or other close relative differs from that of a mere acquaintance). While we may feel the loss keenly, others who do not have strong affectional ties with the deceased experience a "low" kind of grief.

music: the vocal or instrumental pieces that commonly set the tone for the funeral services. Most parishes provide a list of appropriate hymns for the funeral liturgy. Secular music is to be avoided as inappropriate for the sacredness of the actions taking place.

Our Father: the Lord's Prayer. There are seven petitions in this prayer to which the bereaved and grief-stricken can easily relate.

procession: the movement to different stations or moments in the funeral service. Psalms and sacred music generally accompany all who process.

support group: a mutual help group which works with aspects of the grieving process. Members in a parish support group explore the emotional, physical and especially the spiritual dimensions to loss as they assist those who are grieving to work through their loss.

vigil: ritual devotions observed on the eve of the funeral; previously called the wake. It has special prayers for the deceased recited either in the parish church or at the funeral parlor.

Bibliography

Resources for Bereavement

Clinebell, Howard. *Basic Types of Pastoral Care Counseling: Resources for the Ministry of Healing and Growth,* Abingdon Press, Nashville, 1966 & 1984.

Curley, Terence P. *The Ministry of Consolation: A Parish Guide for Comforting the Bereaved,* Alba House, New York, 1993.

_____. *Healing The Broken-Hearted: Consoling the Grief-Stricken,* Alba House, New York, 1995.

_____. *Six Steps for Managing Loss: A Catholic Guide Through Grief,* Alba House, New York, 1997.

_____. "A Bill of Rights for the Bereaved," *Pastoral Life,* Vol. 49, No. 1, January, 2000.

Deits, Bob. *Life After Loss: A Personal Guide Dealing With Death, Divorce, Job Change and Relocation,* Fisher Books, Tucson, AZ, 1988.

Gerkin, Charles V. *Crisis Experience In Modern Life: Theory and Theology of Pastoral Care,* Abingdon Press, Nashville, TN, 1979.

Gilbert, Richard B. *HeartPeace: Healing Help for Grieving Folks,* Abbey Press, St. Meinrad, IN, 1996.

Gilmour, Peter, ed. *Now and at the Hour of Our Death,* Liturgy Training Publications, Chicago, IL, 1989.

Manning, Doug. *Don't Take Away My Grief: What to Do When You Lose a Loved One,* Harper-Collins Publishers, NY, 1979 &1984.

Mitchell, Kenneth R. & Herbert Anderson. *All Our Losses, All*

Our Griefs: Resources for Pastoral Care, Westminster Press, Philadelphia, PA, 1983.

Reilly, Donna & JoAnn Sturzl. *Grief Ministry: Helping Others Mourn,* Resource Publications, San Jose, CA, 1992.

Funeral Liturgy

Boadt, Lawrence, Mary Dombeck, and H. Richard Rutherford. *The Rites of Death and Dying,* 1987, National Meeting of the Federation of Diocesan Liturgical Committees, Liturgical Press, Collegeville, MN, 1988.

Catholic Conference of Canadian Bishops. "The Christian Funeral," *National Bulletin on Liturgy,* 22, No. 119 (197-257), Dec., 1989.

Curley, Terence P. *Console One Another: A Guide to Christian Funerals,* Sheed & Ward, Kansas City, MO, 1993.

_____. "Cremation and Bodily Resurrection," *The Priest,* Vol. 55, No. 4, April, 1999.

_____. "The Order of Christian Funerals: A Better Connection for Pastoral Care," *The Priest,* Vol. 47, No. 4, April, 1991.

_____. "The Tenth Anniversary of the Funeral Ritual," *Pastoral Life,* Vol. 49, No. 4., April, 2000.

_____. "Bringing Order to Funerals," *The Priest,* Vol. 56, No. 3, March, 2000.

International Commission on English in Liturgy (ICEL), *Order of Christian Funerals,* Washington, DC, 1989.

_____. *Order of Christian Funerals, Appendix 2: Cremation,* Catholic Book Publishing Co., Totowa, NJ, 1997.

Rutherford, H. Richard. *The Death of a Christian,* Liturgical Press, Collegeville, MN, 1990.

Spakes, Robert and Richard Rutherford. "The Order of Christian Funerals: A Study in Bereavement and Lament," *Worship,* 60, No. 6, 1986 (499).

Catechetical Formation & Instruction

Curley, Terence P. "The Catechism of the Catholic Church, A Resource for Pastoral Life," *The Priest,* Vol. 49, No. 6, June, 1993.

_____. "The New Catechism and the RCIA Journey," *Pastoral Life,* Vol. 44, No. 2, February, 1994.

_____. "*Veritatis Splendor* as Spiritual Direction," *Pastoral Life,* Vol. 43, No. 8, Sept., 1994.

_____. "*Evangelium Vitae* and Our Culture," *The Priest,* Vol. 51, No. 10, October, 1995.

_____. "The Pursuit of Truth," Viewpoint, *The Priest,* Vol. 55, No. 7, July, 1999.

_____. "The Office for the Dead: A Parish Prayer," *The Priest,* Vol. 52, No. 11, Nov., 1996.

_____. "Spiritual Steps for Managing Loss," *Pastoral Life,* Vol. 47, No. 11, 1998.

U.S. Catholic Conference. *Catechism of the Catholic Church,* Doubleday, New York, 1984.

_____. *Our Hearts Were Burning Within Us,* Committee on Education, U.S. Catholic Conference, Washington, DC, 1999.

Hardon, John, S.J. *The Question and Answer Catholic Catechism,* Doubleday, New York, 1981.

Lawler, Ronald, Donald W. Wuerl, Thomas C. Lawler. *The Teaching of Christ: A Catholic Catechism for Adults,* Our Sunday Visitor, Huntington, IN, 1979.

McBride, Alfred. *Father McBride's Family Catechism,* Our Sunday Visitor, Huntington, IN, 1987.

Pennock, Michael. *This Is Our Faith: A Catholic Catechism for Adults,* Ave Maria Press, Notre Dame, IN, 1989.

Psalms

Anderson, Bernhard W. *Out of the Depths: The Psalms Speak for Us Today,* Westminster Press, Philadelphia, PA, 1983.

Brueggemann, Walter. *The Message of the Psalms: A Theological Commentary*, Augsburg Publishing Co., Minneapolis, MN, 1984.

Craghan, John F. *Psalms for all Seasons,* Liturgical Press, Collegeville, MN, 1993.

Creach, Jerome F.D., *Psalms,* Interpretation Bible Studies, Geneva Press, Kentucky, 1998.

Dollen, Charles. *Prayerbook of the King: The Psalms,* Alba House, New York, 1998.

Quillo, Ronald. *The Psalms: Prayers of Many Moods,* Paulist Press, Mahwah, NJ, 1998.

Grief Support

Curley, Terence P. *A Way of the Cross for the Bereaved,* Alba House, New York, 1996.

Ministry of Consolation Training Manual, National Catholic Ministry to the Bereaved. For further information contact the Office of the National Catholic Ministry to the Bereaved, 28700 Euclid Ave., Cleveland, OH (440) 943-3480.

Gilbert, Richard B. *Finding Your Way After Your Parent Dies,* Ave Maria Press, Notre Dame, IN, 1999.

O'Brien, Maureen. *Praying Through Grief: Healing Prayer Services for Those Who Mourn,* Ave Maria Press, Notre Dame, IN, 1997.

_____. *The New Day Journal: A Journey from Grief to Healing,* ACTA Publications, Chicago, IL, 2000.

Audio-Visual Guides for Good Grief

The Following Audio-Visuals are by Father Terence P. Curley

From Darkness to Light: A Healing Path Through Grief, Alba House Communications, Canfield, OH. This is a four-part audio program which provides the listener with healing ways to go through grief. The tapes provide an overview of the grieving process, an explanation of symptoms, and helpful ways to place the loss into the context of faith.

Through the Dark Valley: Healing Steps for Managing Loss, Alba House Communications, Canfield, OH. This four-part video presentation further explains Father Curley's title *Six Steps for Managing Loss*. The presentation gives effective steps for managing our losses. It develops a spirituality for those who are grieving.

Journey To Healing: A Ministry For The Bereaved, Alba House Communications, Canfield, OH. This four-part video is used as an introduction for grief ministers, support groups, bereavement committees, and those who are grieving. It provides insights into the dynamics of taking the journey through grief.

Arise & Walk: A Christian Grieving Guide, Alba House Communications, Canfield, OH. This is a four-part video which provides guidance for going through grief. The video highlights insights for a Christian spirituality for loss.

(All of the above are also available through Andrew Lane Co., 800-451-2520)

ST PAULS

This book was designed and published by St. Pauls/
Alba House, the publishing arm of the Society of St.
Paul, an international religious congregation of priests
and brothers dedicated to serving the Church through
the communications media. For information regarding
this and associated ministries of the Pauline Family of
Congregations, write to the Vocation Director, Society
of St. Paul, 7050 Pinehurst, Dearborn, Michigan 48126.
Phone (313) 582-3798 or check our internet site,
www.albahouse.org